DON'T WEAR YOUR GI TO THE BAR AND OTHER JIU-JITSU LIFE LESSONS

MARSHAL D. CARPER
&
DARRYL COZZA

ARTÈCHOKE MEDIA

PITTSBURGH, PA

CONTENTS

Introduction

Preface

This book is for entertainment purposes only. Any similarities to persons living or dead is coincidental. Martial arts is a dangerous physical activity that should only be practiced under the supervision of an experienced instructor. Due to the intensity of martial arts, you should consult your doctor before training a martial art or before trying any of the techniques in this book.

Authors' note: All techniques and scenarios were simulated in a high-tech training laboratory. Do not attempt to recreate these simulations at home.

Why BJJ Doesn't Work

Don't wear your gi to the bar.

M That's your first jiu-jitsu life lesson. Like the best of us, you probably think that your gi is the coolest piece of clothing that you own. It's your suit of armor. It carries your blood, your sweat, your tears, and your passion. Your school patches are on the lapels and across your back, and the fabric at the knees is frayed and discolored from months and months of mat work. You think that your gi is the coolest piece of clothing that you own because it is. Jiu-jitsu has been scientifically proven in numerous peer reviewed studies to be the greatest invention modern man has ever known.

Unfortunately, not everyone agrees. The masses have yet to see that jiu-jitsu could be the force that solves world hunger, ends poverty, and brings about world peace. They do not understand it.

When you tell them what jiu-jitsu is and how often you train, they shake their heads and shuffle off to watch the next season of *Survivor* while you perfect your new favorite move.

And this is why you don't wear your gi to the bar. In a world of Jiu-Jitsu Enlightenment, which is the period of prosperity that will follow the Jiu-Jitsu Renaissance that Leonardo Da Vinci predicted in one of his many journal entries, wearing your gi to the bar would guarantee you free drinks and an endless number of suitors. Not so in our troubled society.

If you wear your gi to the bar in today's socio-economic climate, you will be met with quizzical stares. The resident tough guys will challenge you to a fight, the girls will scoff, and the bouncer will impolitely ask you to leave. In the worst cases, you will be immediately attacked by a swarm of twelve year olds from the closest Tae Kwon Do school who, through sheer numbers, subdue you and revoke your man card.

This is all completely true because my coauthor, Darryl Cozza, and I have tried it multiple times in the name of jiu-jitsu science, and we bring our findings to you so that you may use our knowledge to overcome the obstacles we faced and to develop new knowledge. And so jiu-jitsu continues to grow.

As you read through the four sections—why Brazilian Jiu-Jitsu doesn't work, how to explain jiu-jitsu to non-jiteiros, jiu-jitsu for the street, and on the mat wisdom—take notes. Meditate on the parables and the metaphors. Ask a holy man to guide you through the spiritual awakening that this book will inevitably trigger.

Just kidding.

Do not take this book too seriously. It's like a friendly roll: part serious, part experimental, and part humor. We hope that you have as much fun reading it as we did writing it.

* * * * *

All jiu-jiteiros, from white belts to black belts, will face the same challenge many times over: haters, doubters, critics, and martial-arts-ignorant-buffoons. These individuals can smell a jiu-jiteiro. You may try to hide, but they will find you. In your cubicle. At a backyard barbeque. At the bar. At a reunion. At Comic-Con. They will waddle right up to you, stand inches from your face, and grin.

They will say, "Brazilian Jiu-Jitsu doesn't work."

And they will keep grinning, gazing into your jiu-jiteiro soul, waiting for you to react.

No one can explain why this happens, and many have tried. The Super Secret Brazilian Jiu-Jitsu Reseach Center, housed in the left hand of the Rio de Janeiro Jesus statue—the Super Secret Brazilian Soccer Research Center is in the right hand—has been researching this phenomena for decades and has yet to determine a conclusive cause. All we know is that the first recorded sighting of jiu-jitsu doubters was in 1929, the year that Helio Gracie taught his first jiu-jitsu class. For decades, jiu-jitsu doubters were mostly limited to the streets and beaches of Brazil, where they were quickly dispatched by one of the miscellaneous Gracie family members. If the doubter was an exceptionally tough case, Helio and Carlos would simultaneously input their respective launch codes and unleash Rickson Gracie.

Cases of jiu-jitsu doubt did not reach epidemic levels until the invention of the Internet, at which point YouTube made every mouse jockey a keyboard warrior and martial arts expert. Now, no jiu-jiteiro is safe. Doubters can appear at any time, and if you have any hope of ever being worth the third-world child labor that stitched your belt, you have to be ready to act.

Take this true story for example:

I was working in West Virginia. In short, I was an office drone. One of my coworkers, a bumbling brunette that was worshipped by the other drones in what can be described as a sausage-saturated environment, was married to a West Virginia State Police cadet. He came in one Saturday to help with a community outreach event that we hosted. Until then, we had been friendly. We laughed at each other's jokes, made small talk, and generally coexisted without incident. We will call him Scott.

This day was different.

Scott had just completed two weeks of personal tactics training, a total of 80 hours of self-defense if he was training non-stop, which is unlikely. Wanting to keep the tone for the day upbeat and friendly, I asked Scott about what his training entailed, being genuinely interested in what State Police would cram into a hand-to-hand crash course to prepare its cadets for West Virginia's worst.

Scott demonstrated a bear hug escape on his girlfriend—a dubious technique that hinged upon rapping his attacker's knuckles with his knuckles—and said, "A lot of street ready tactics like that."

The brunette said, "It's crazy how effective that is."

I hid my skepticism and said that it was interesting. Scott sat down in front of me, leaned in, and grinned. I should have seen the symptoms, but maybe my recent knee surgery or my belief in the intelligence of the West Virginia State Police clouded my judgment.

Scott said, "And they taught us how to beat guys like you."

"Guys like me?"

"Guys like you."

"In two weeks?"

Scott kept grinning. "Yeah," he said. "A quick eye gouge or groin shot shuts down you jiu-jitsu guys right away."

Like any jiu-jiteiro caught off guard, I fumed. I raged. I looked to the heavens and called upon Helio Gracie to save the soul of this lost self-defense sheep… in my head of course. Externally, I did my best to maintain my composure.

"You're right. Your two weeks would beat my six years any day. Just remember your training when some hillbilly wrestler changes levels on you," I said.

"Changes what?"

"You'll know what I mean when you see it."

And from that day on, office life was uncomfortable. As Scott neared his graduation, returning to the office in various stages of his State Police uniform, worship of his power and his combat abilities grew. My fellow drones asked jokingly but seriously for Scott to have mercy on them, and the brunette jokingly but seriously threatened to "call Scott" on anyone that crossed her. This continued after Scott graduated and worsened when he came in to show off his police issue Glock and snazzy flat brimmed, leather chin-strapped State Police hat. He even began to call himself Trooper Scott, talking in the third person when he did so.

Trooper Scott, unfortunately, is not a one-of-a-kind knuckle dragger, but he is an oddity as far as law enforcement is concerned. Police officers, in general, do not tend to be doubters, especially with the prevalence of the Gracie Combatives curriculum. One of my instructors is a police officer, and many of my training partners are police officers. They get it. Trooper Scott will probably never get it, even when he happens upon a coked-out redneck that wrestled in middle school and remembers a picture-perfect fireman's carry in the midst of resisting arrest.

If you, dear reader, are ever in West Virginia and are pulled over by

Trooper Scott (see the provided videos so that you can identify him), please tell him that you know me. Tell him that he is a fool for doubting Brazilian Jiu-Jitsu and that you would be happy to choke him out to prove to him that his two weeks of training has not prepared him to beat a bona fide jiu-jiteiro. Then calmly step out of your car, put on your gi, and get down to business.

On second thought, no, do not do that. Trooper Scott carries a gun and may be emotionally unstable and unpredictable. Just obey the speed limit and do not do any drugs when you are in West Virginia.

The rest of this chapter will address various jiu-jitsu doubt scenarios and how you can respond to and diffuse Trooper Scott-esque situations. The most satisfying conclusion would be for the doubter to visit your gym and train with you, your training partners, and your instructor. Disclaimer: this will never happen. Instead, you will be satisfied in knowing that you presented a logical argument on behalf of your art. A doubter will ignore every point that you make, of course. The validity of your points will always be irrelevant, but you will at least have some satisfaction.

For your own sanity, though, you need to know how to counter their arguments in the very rare event that you could convert the doubter into a believer and invite him to join our order. In this chapter, we will address the most common arguments for why jiu-jitsu is not effective, and explain why these arguments are nothing but cow pucky.

The Ground is Not Your Friend

The scenario:

You are in a dark alley. Dumpsters. Trash bags. Those wooden palette things leaning against a graffiti brick wall. And it happens: a mugger emerges from the shadows. He demands your wallet

Simulated thug encounter.

Our research indicates that eye-patch wearing, cigarette-smoking thugs can be particularly quarrelsome.

and your life. It's okay. You have been training for this.

You are a purple belt in Brazilian Jiu-Jitsu. You have gone to seminars.

You know how to fight.

He does not have a weapon, and he is not that much bigger than you.

Your jiu-jitsu should make quick work of this alley-camping thug. All you have

to do is pull guard and everything will be fine. Just grab his sleeve and throw your legs around his

waist and land on the ground...

. . . that is covered in broken glass! The ground is covered in broken glass! The guy at your office that does Aikido told you that this day would come. He stood by the printer, rubbing his pot belly, and said that you would never want to take a street fight to the ground because you would be fighting on pavement, or gravel, or glass, or lava, or pigmy goats. A thug is about to take your wallet and your life, and you are going to scuff your knees and ruin your brand new wife beater (if you are wearing a TapouT t-shirt, you already lost). Your guard is unstoppable in the gym, but this unfortunate terrain is not soft. Your jiu-jitsu is worthless without 1.5 inches of foam padding beneath your feet.

Had you heeded Office Aikido Guy's advice, you could catch the thug's right cross with both hands and use a wrist lock to flip him into one of the dumpsters. If you had learned Tae Kwon Do, you could break one of the palettes in half with your fist and use it as a shield. But no, you bought into the hype. You trained Gracie Jiu-Jitsu. None of the Bully Prevention DVDs taught you how to fight on broken glass.

Then it hits you. You took this one class where you did not learn to fight from guard. You learned about this thing called a takedown. Fortunately,

when you finish a takedown, your attacker lands on his back, which in this realer than real scenario, puts his body between you and the broken glass. From there, you can knee on belly until he gives you his wallet and apologizes for contributing to the decay of urban America. If takedowns are not part of your street jiu-jitsu, we have provided a step-by-step breakdown of a basic takedown.

The explanation:

The guard is what made jiu-jitsu famous. Many of us were drawn to the mat after seeing Royce Gracie finish ogre after ogre from his back in the first few Ultimate Fighting Championships. The mechanics of the guard in all of its beautiful complexity fascinates us, and we enjoy experimenting with new and innovative ways of entangling and ensnaring our opponents with our guard. We lasso. We invert. We bait. We feint. The guard is an amazing position, and there is no feeling quite like the one you get when you finish someone from your guard.

However, no sane jiu-jiteiro would ever choose to fight from guard in any sort of street confrontation. If you asked him, he would say, "Back mount, please"—or if he has a flare for hitting people—"Mount, please."

Position is king, and when strikes are involved, being on top will always be superior to being on bottom. When you are in the top position, gravity increases your leverage, allowing you to use your weight as well as your limbs to stifle and control your opponent as you hunt for the finish, an advantage that you do not have on your back. Furthermore, gravity automatically makes your strikes stronger, and you can create and eliminate space to protect yourself from strikes. Top positions are better for self-defense. This is common knowledge in the grappling world.

We do not practice the guard because we plan on busting out reverse de la Riva in the middle of a mugging. We practice the guard because we want to be prepared in the event that we are forced into an unfavorable position. If we end up on our backs, we want to know exactly what to do to protect ourselves to either end the fight or reverse the position. This same reasoning justifies our practice of escapes and counters. We never want to be in a headlock, but knowing how to escape has obvious practical value.

In sport jiu-jitsu, we use a variety of guards because it is fun, and the advanced mastery of leverage and control is necessary when competing against other high-level grapplers. An untrained attacker will quickly make a novice mistake, exposing himself to a submission. High-level grapplers do not make these mistakes, so more complex strategies and tactics come into play. To put it in terms that a non-grappler might understand: the rope-a-dope strategy that made Muhammad Ali famous and successful required an advanced understanding and application of boxing mechanics. Would the rope-a-dope be practical in a bar fight? Certainly not. Would a boxer of Muhammad Ali's caliber have any problem out-striking anyone that was not also a world-class boxer? Certainly not. A highly evolved opponent warranted a highly evolved strategy, and the highly evolved strategy in no way negates the effectiveness of the art.

The other misconception contributing to this argument against jiu-jitsu, besides the notion that you would not want to pull guard in a street fight, is that the ground in the street is dirty and wrought with peril, nothing like a soft and inviting gym mat. This is true, but this is really more of an argument for jiu-jitsu than it is against. If you watch the *Gracie Jiu-Jitsu in Action DVDs,* you can see a string of matches against Karate experts taking place on what looks like hardwood floors. Being on the wrong end of a hip throw when hardwood flooring is involved sucks, which is more of an advantage for the grappler than it is for the non-grappler.

If the ground is an undesirable place to be, who is more prepared to dictate whether or not the fight goes there? The grappler who has spent

Marshal convinces the thug to go back to school. He lends him a book and writes him a letter of recommendation.

countless hours practicing takedowns as well as takedown defense or the non-grappler with no takedown experience at all?

If the fight is taken to the ground, who is more likely to be on top and thus relatively safe from the perils of the surface for the majority of the fight? The grappler who has spent countless hours perfecting his ability to achieve and maintain dominant position against a resisting opponent or the non-grappler with no such experience?

My point should already be clear, but I will spell it out. Training jiu-jitsu gives you the ability to choose where the fight takes place. If you decide that you want to take the fight to the ground but would prefer not to have your back on pavement, you can execute a takedown and land on top, where you at worst scuff your knees. If you decide that you would prefer not to take the fight to the ground for any number of reasons, you have enough training to maintain your footing and continue fighting, especially if a larger opponent is attempting to caveman you. Anyone that has trained any portion of the Gracie self-defense curriculum or something similar knows that Brazilian Jiu-Jitsu also incorporates a fair amount of stand-up techniques for this very reason. A complete jiu-jitsu fighter is proficient in striking, both in and out of the clinch, and can finish the fight from standing as well.

The notion that jiu-jitsu is ineffective because you would not want to fight from your back in the street is based on two very wrong misconceptions: that you would want to play guard in the first place and that you would always choose to take the fight to the ground. When Office Aikido Guy throws this argument at you, sit him down and show him the truth.

How to Triangle Choke Multiple Opponents

The scenario:

You are riding your bike home in the dark, and a gang of students from a rival martial arts school has just left a Halloween dance and is chasing you down a gravel road. No, no, no. That's overdone.

Okay, picture this. You are walking to your car after another day of watching jiu-jitsu videos on YouTube when you were supposed to be slogging through a database updating entries and crunching numbers. You have your earbuds in and are listening to Gracie Jiu-Jitsu motivational mp3s. Your stroll is happy and, dare I say, perky. Work is over, and an enjoyable training session is next on the agenda. As you near your car, you notice a few shadows slinking in your well-trained peripheral vision.

Four attackers materialize, and they are armed. They demand that you burn them a copy of your motivational mp3s or else they will inflict bodily harm. As an upstanding citizen, you know that burning a copy of the files is out of the question. Copyright infringement is illegal, and you would never willfully pirate or facilitate the pirating of a jiu-jitsu related product. Therefore, your life is now in danger.

In the gym, you only ever fight one person at a time. You touch hands,

MULTIPLE ATTACKERS. ONE BAD ASS JIU-JITERIO.
Artéchoke Films Presents :
"SWEEP THEM ALL!"
starring
Marshal D. Carper
FEATURING KOUNT KOZA & THE KUNG FU KLAW!

start from your knees, and fumble your way to patty-caking into a submission—with one dude. Now, you are facing four guys and their weapons. If you had trained Tae Kwon Do, you could high kick your way out of danger and end the fight. If you had trained Krav Maga, you would methodically remove the innards of each attacker and mount them at the gates of your city. But you chose to train the lowly art of Brazilian Jiu-Jitsu. How could you ever take each attacker to the ground and submit them one at a time without getting your head kicked in?

The explanation:

No martial art can guarantee that you will be on the winning end of a multiple-attacker encounter. Any martial art or martial arts instructor that claims differently is lying. Coming out ahead against more than one opponent, even when you have a gun, is a feat. The reality of the circumstances is painful: you are one person with two arms and two legs. As soon as a second attacker enters the equation, you are at a significant disadvantage. When you dedicate any attention to one opponent, you are vulnerable to an attack from the second. If a third or a fourth attacker is involved, the odds very quickly swing even farther from your favor.

You are not Jason Bourne. Hacking your way through wave after wave of bad guys is a dream that all of us share, but it is not practical nor is it ethical to convince someone that a martial art will give them the skills to consistently survive a scenario against more than one opponent.

A legitimate martial arts instructor of any discipline will disclose this cold equation and do so willingly. Even after years of training, you are still a human, and humans are ultimately fragile creatures. One unexpected strike is all it takes to end a fight, and with more than two limbs flailing at you, the chances of you eating a punch are great. Shortly after your legitimate martial arts instructor explains this, he will proceed to tell you about the importance of prevention and situational awareness.

Avoiding dangerous situations is point number one of any serious self-defense curriculum, and it is an important aspect of jiu-jitsu for self-defense. Jiu-jiteiros think about life in terms of leverage, the greatest gain possible achieved with the least amount of effort. In a self-defense scenario where the stakes could be your life, the most effective technique is to never enter into such a situation in the first place. The tactics necessary for accomplishing this are common sense and fairly well-known, but they are worth repeating.

Know your surroundings. If you are in a high-crime zone, park in the safest, well-lit areas possible. Avoid traveling alone, especially late at night and when you are passing through areas that make great ambush points. If you are attacked, there is nothing shameful about high-tailing it out of there, especially if a weapon or more than one person is involved.

Common sense, situational awareness, and a reasonable amount of preparation can spare you more confrontation than any single self-defense technique. We are going to release a DVD series that says this and charge $300.00 because so few people understand this. If you don't, get your credit card. If you have a friend or a foe that doesn't, get his credit card. Buy him ten copies of this book and pre-order the DVD. Buy yourself something nice too.

With the "the best way to win a fight is to avoid a fight" speech out of the way, the one you give to your ugly children (pretty kids don't get beat up), we can address the practical application of Brazilian Jiu-Jitsu in a street fight with multiple attackers.

First thing: a self-defense-oriented jiu-jitsu curriculum addresses striking, both offensively and defensively. We do not attempt to reach the striking prowess of a boxer because in our system bludgeoning someone to death or into submission is not typically an efficient way of ending a fight.

Hands are made of small bones and are not really designed to strike hard objects repeatedly, and every second we spend swinging away at an attacker is an opportunity for him to swing back. If we close the distance and enter a clinch or take him down, we can avoid getting hit and can instead put him to sleep. Choking someone out is so much cleaner, and you do not have to explain to a judge why you felt it necessary to turn his face into a strawberry snow cone.

In a street fight, there are far too many fists and feet for you to go toe-to-toe with everyone. Some push kicks and some defensive footwork are a great way to (try to) maintain some distance as you attempt to run. But what if someone grabs you? Well hot damn, it's a good thing you picked a martial art that focuses exclusively on what to do if someone grabs you. After a few years of doing jiu-jitsu, you will be pretty good at wiggling out of any hold or grip (assuming you were smart enough to put on a gi) a riff raff street rat can throw your way.

And this is where jiu-jitsu really shines: in a multiple attacker scenario you are in the most danger when someone attempts to restrain you. Jiu-jitsu makes you really good at dealing with the worst possible scenario. If you are really afraid of multiple attackers, and that is what inspires you to train martial arts, you should train Brazilian Jiu-Jitsu, and you should jog every once a while and mix in some sprints.

Please, No, Not in the Face (or the Groin, Thanks)

The scenario:

The fight is on. You wanted to sell your old mattress and box spring because you planned on upgrading to a Hampton hotel-style mattress and mattress pad. It's like sleeping on a cloud, and when your hobby is getting thrown and squished by grown men, you like to come home to something soft and nonthreatening.

You met him in a Walmart parking lot, a usual place for a Craigslist

Marshal demonstrates that having the superior position—
one of the core concepts of jiu-jitsu—not only protects you from eye
gouges and groin strikes but also puts you in a position to use them.

meeting that did not start on the Missed Connections board, and he seemed reasonable. He evaluated your wares, looking for stains, tears, and damage. You're no crook. The items are in mint condition, and your price is fair. But he starts jerking you around.

"There's a ding here. Did you see this ding? It's definitely dinged," he says. "The price has to come down."

You examine the alleged ding, and you disagree. The integrity of the item is in no way compromised, and a fitted sheet will cover it right up. No, the price is not changing. If you go any lower, you will have lost money on the gas it took to drive here in the first place.

"It's dinged pretty bad. Can't do it, man."

You argue. He begins to shout. He gestures angrily. You gesture back. The underpaid grunt collecting lost shopping carts stares at the two of

you suspiciously, the sun glinting off of his neon green reflective vest.

You decide that you do not deserve this. You turn to leave, but he grabs you. Your instincts take over, and you execute a quick hip throw, dropping him on to the pavement. You immediately establish position and work to control him, but his rage is driving him to madness. Foam leaks from his mouth. His eyes are wide, unblinking. This Craigslist encounter gone wrong has brought out the worst in this man. He is devolving before your eyes, becoming a cornered, frenzied beast.

You slide to mount, and then it happens. With one hand, he grips your scrotum, squeezing with *Blood Sport* fury, his fingernails ripping through your jeans. With his other hand, he rakes your eyes. You have lost. Your vision is gone, and your manhood is defiled. You could have avoided this fate, and here is how.

The explanation:

Non-jiu-jiteiros assume that executing an eye-gouge or a groin-strike in a fight is easy, and that it is even easier against a grappler who has chosen to remain close to you, rather than bouncing in and out of striking range like a kickboxer might. This belief is incredibly common, and it is not an unreasonable assumption for a non-grappler to make. It's wrong, absolutely wrong, but you should be able to see how the uninitiated would arrive at this conclusion.

Generally, self-defense seminars are to blame. Most people are exposed to self-defense at some point in their lives, in gym class or from a friend that tells them to carry their keys between their fingers, and most of these exposures advocate eye-gouges and groin-strikes. The reasoning is simple: a blind attacker cannot fight, and when at a physical disadvantage, the groin represents a vulnerable, high-pain-inducing target. When weighing the effectiveness of eye-gouging and groin-strikes, consider these points:

1. A groin-strike may not be enough to stop an attacker, especially if your aim is poor.

2. A self-defense plan focused on striking the groin is useless as soon as the groin is out of range.

3. The eyes are very small targets and thus can be difficult to attack.

4. If you believe in the effectiveness of eye-gouging, you must be fully prepared to blind your opponent, which requires some extreme digging.

5. Initiating an eye-gouge or a groin-strike can give your attacker the idea to do the same, which will likely end badly for you if you are already at a physical or positional disadvantage.

6. Practicing eye-gouges and groins-strikes is incredibly impractical, so it can be difficult to get good at them.

Before I delve any deeper into this topic, we need to address an issue that lurks beneath the surface of this topic. Advocates of eye-gouging and groin-striking ultimately assume that a quick fix, an instant solution, exists for self-defense. These are the same people that believe an hour-long seminar on self-defense is enough to prepare an individual to react appropriately when their life is in danger. There are no quick fixes. A fight is comprised of far too many variables for a short primer on self-defense to be effective. Self-defense requires a great deal of practice, which develops awareness, technique, and the ability to improvise. This is why many police officers choose to train a martial art after they graduate from the academy, and it's also why the military never stops practicing. Learning what to do is the easy part. Getting really good at it is the important part, and that takes time.

In jiu-jitsu, we are constantly talking about control—controlling our breathing, controlling the space, controlling our opponent—and this is for good reason. Chaos is dangerous. We need to be calm, and we need to be aware of what is happening in a fight so that we can make the right decisions. If we clinch with an attacker, for example, we remove many of the unknowns. Not only can we feel our opponent attempting to move, giving us a direct connection to their intentions, we can use the lack of space to protect ourselves from wild haymakers while we methodically improve our position.

This control also allows us to manage the seriousness of the fight. In a fight, you might not always desire to maim your opponent. It may be better to subdue them until the police (or the bouncers) arrive. If you escalate the intensity of the violence, you could actually make the situation worse, which is incredibly inefficient if all you really needed to do was pin your attacker and calm him down. Furthermore, you may need to justify your level of force in court.

"Well, you see, Your Honor, he was trying to steal my Pokémon cards, so I put him in this thing called a twister, which is actually a wrestler's guillotine. I mean, they're the same thing, but Eddie Bravo learned the wrestler's guillotine while he wrestled, and then when he started using it in jiu-jitsu it started to be called the twister, probably because there's already another move called a guillotine. Anyway, he was stealing my favorite Charizard card, and by "he" I mean this guy here and not Eddie Bravo. Eddie Bravo would never steal my Pokémon cards. So I took him down, and I used a twister to end the fight, which is probably why he is paralyzed now and has to poop into a bag."

Justifying scooping out an eyeball would be just as difficult.

Jiu-jitsu gives you the ability to choose how much force you need to end a fight. You do not have to hit them until their face is the consistency of extra-crunchy peanut butter, but it's an option if you deem it necessary. You do not have to rip out their shoulder and dislocate their elbow, but that too is an option if you deem it necessary. And you do not have to choke them unconscious, but it's an option if you feel as though pain compliance would be ineffective or unnecessarily messy or simply take too long. Note: let go when they pass out, but position them so that they can easily be restrained until the police arrive... or just book it out of there.

Going right for the eyes or the groin immediately escalates the situation to life or death, which can work against you in a mugging as well as a bar fight.

As for eye-gouging and groin-strikes being the quick and simple way to nullify jiu-jitsu—as Trooper Scott would have you believe—that's nonsense, and there's more to the nonsense than the points I have already made.

In jiu-jitsu, position is king. If you are in a dominant position, your eyes and groin are actually inaccessible in most cases. In the few cases where your opponent could reach your eyes and groin, his ability to do so is still limited while you can easily pluck out both of his eyes. This harkens back to an earlier point: initiating an eye gouge gives your attacker the same idea, which is very bad if he is in a better position to eye gouge than you are.

When your position is dominant, there is either too little space for your opponent to eye-gouge or groin-strike, or is he is at such a disadvantage that his attempts to eye-gouge or groin-strike could be easily countered with a fight-ending submission or a brutal strike. To jiu-jiteiros, this is obvious. The power of effective positioning is clear to us because we experience it every day, but to outsiders this point will be difficult to grasp. Rather than continuing to argue the virtues of position and control, which will do little to convince a doubter, we have prepared a video that demonstrates this concept, which should put the issue of eye-gouging and groin-striking to rest. Oh, and this counts for biting too, you cannibal.

Marshal demonstrates that having the superior position—
one of the core concepts of jiu-jitsu—not only protects you from eye
gouges and groin strikes but also puts you in a position to use them.

"My Boyfriend Lifts a Lot of Weights"

The scenario:

You are at a party with your girlfriend. Her friends. All of your friends are pitching in for a pay-per-view, and since jiu-jiteiros are notoriously broke, 43 friends are cramming into a basement to watch the fights. Your absence caused panic. Nobody was sure how to divide up the remaining dollar, forcing your gym to host an in-house tournament to determine who would pay and who would not. You tried to prevent it, you tried to attend, but you had no choice. You never hang out with her friends, and you are always at the gym. You owe her this, and you know it. It's only fair, and if you can't see that you should really be asking yourself why you're in this relationship at all.

Her words, not yours.

You follow your girlfriend from clique to clique, meeting people and promptly forgetting their names. No matter. After the introductions, you stand there silently while your girlfriend shares inside jokes with friends and coworkers. You sip your beer and smile, glancing around at the small army of non-jiteiros in the room, occasionally checking your phone for updates on the fights.

"He does what?"

"It's called jiu-jitsu," your girlfriend says.

"I've never heard of that," an over-tanned blonde replies. She looks at you. "Is that like training UFC?"

"Something like that, yeah."

"How is that fun?"

"The technique involved is actually pretty interesting. It's really cool how leverage and strategy can help a little guy to beat a little guy. That's what makes it fun," you say.

"Do you think you could beat my boyfriend up?" the blonde asks.

"What?"

"Could you beat him up? He body builds. He's really strong."

You hesitate, unsure of how best to navigate the many verbal booby-traps set out before you.

"I don't think you could. He is a lot bigger than you." She points to a man across the room. His biceps are as thick as your waist. "That's him."

You feel your girlfriend looking at you, and when you turn to face her, her eyes burrow into your mind. Somehow, she uses the darkness of her pupils to plant a message in your brain. The message reads:

"Keep your damn mouth shut. We hardly ever go out, and I just want to have fun, just this once. Don't ruin this for me. Do not start shit with my friends. I. Will. Kill. You."

You turn back to face the blonde. "Yeah, he does look strong." Then you excuse yourself to refill your drink. As you walk toward the refrigerator, you chug the remainder of your beer and envision what could have been.

The explanation:

The effectiveness of technique is alien to anyone that has not been thrashed by a high level grappler half their size. Even when you know jiu-jitsu, a flyweight phenom that tosses you around like a cat toying with a dead mouse is an amazing feeling. It's painful, but it reminds you how powerful jiu-jitsu can be. Convincing someone who has no real interest in visiting a gym and trying jiu-jitsu that technique can overcome strength is difficult if not impossible. Feeling is believing, and you are not going to demonstrate moves at a party. Carpet burn is no fun, and a demonstration is liable to morph into an impromptu sparring match

While simulated bodybuilder worked on this....

Marshal worked on this....

as they resist more and more to prove that you could not finish them if they were actually fighting back (speaking from experience here).

So how do you convince someone that jiu-jitsu can beat biceps without actually starting a fight?

My go to maneuver is to load up some Marcelo Garcia highlights to demonstrate how a small fighter can overcome a significant weight disadvantage, and when the argument that Garcia isn't striking is presented, I load footage of Royce and Rickson Gracie using jiu-jitsu in the dark ages of mixed martial arts. They had to deal with strikes, and jiu-jitsu still got them the win.

The next obstacle, which is virtually insurmountable without actually sparring, is the "well, that wouldn't happen to me" attitude. They see proof of jiu-jitsu beating boxers, kung fu artists, and wrestlers, but they still believe that it would not work on them. They are simply too strong or too fast or too smart to fall victim to the hocus pocus of jiu-jitsu. After you have presented your arguments and face this challenge, and even arguing at all may be futile, walking away may be the wisest course of action. You would have better luck arguing politics.

While we are on the topic of jiu-jitsu versus muscles, we should explore the common belief that technique always beats strength. This is a half-truth. Ignoring this fact will cause a great deal of heartache.

Yes, technique can beat strength and size, but that does not make it easy. Size and strength are major advantages for those that possess them, and the greater the difference between their physique and yours, the more technique required to overcome the disadvantage. As much as we wish this were not the case, size and strength matter, a lot. Taking on a goliath is not easy, and any veteran jiu-jiteiro should admit this. If that goliath knows some jiu-jitsu, winning becomes even more difficult. Every purple belt knows a white or a blue belt that breaks the scale at 275 pounds or more, and when they have to roll together, the purple belt will undoubtedly sigh deeply, mentally preparing himself for the battle to come.

I belabor this topic because newer students should be aware of this fact. Jiu-jitsu beats inexperienced strength ninety-nine percent of the time. When jiu-jitsu faces jiu-jitsu and strength, the rate of success decreases significantly because athleticism augments the effectiveness of technique. No one would doubt the technical ability of Andre Galvao, but even he admits that strength training and conditioning are essential to his success. At this point in the evolution of the sport, the highest achieving competitors are highly skilled and exceptionally fit. David Levy-Booth, who maintains a great blog called *the Jiu-Jitsu Laboratory*, noted the full consequences of this trend in an article that followed the 2012 Pan Jiu-Jitsu Championships.

In divisions as low as blue belt, the competitors taking first place were professional athletes. They trained full time. They were not stopping by the gym on their way home from the office and then banging out a few work emails while their wives sleep next to them. These are guys that train at least five days a week, perfecting both their technique and their conditioning. If one of these grapplers is paired against a grappler with equal technique but who lacks conditioning, the grappler with the greater conditioning is most likely to win. Technique is still incredibly important, but in a sport setting where the level of technique at the top of each divisions begins to approach equality, other variables become more important. And in reality, this same evolution has occurred in every sport, from football to curling. As a sport becomes more popular, the quality of top competitors improves to the point that the world's best are both highly skilled and physically gifted.

Size and strength do matter, as much as we wish that were not the case. However, the evolution of jiu-jitsu as a sport in no way negates the effectiveness and practicality of jiu-jitsu for self-defense. Against a larger, stronger opponent, jiu-jitsu gives the little guy the best chance of winning, and we have seen jiu-jitsu make the difference in hundreds of scenarios just like this. When someone does not know jiu-jitsu, they quickly make fundamental errors. Without knowledge, strength and size will only delay the inevitable, but we do not recommend embarrassing your girlfriend at parties to prove this point.

Nobody Wears a Gi in the Street

The scenario:

You have just finished a rousing game of racquetball. You walk through the cardio wing, trying not to make eye contact with the StairMaster sisters, and you circumnavigate the free weight pit (the grunting makes you uncomfortable, and the tradition of throwing dumbbells after a set is unnerving). You enter the locker room, averting your eyes from the prehistoric reproductive organs dangling over benches like slain medusas. You undress, strategically facing a corner locker, and scurry to the showers.

In the shower, you thoroughly scrub down. The chances of getting ringworm from a racquetball court are probably pretty low, but a decade of grappling has made you treat every bathing opportunity as a decontamination session. Impetigo, staph, ringworm—they could be hiding in any corner, plotting an attack. Your loofah is your preemptive strike. It cleans and exfoliates in one swoop, uprooting the encampments of bacteria and viruses, executing the ring leaders and liberating the healthy skin cells held prisoner.

As you ponder the merits and complexities of microscopic shower wars, a shadow approaches from behind, but you do not directly acknowledge it. This skill—looking but not looking—is quite useful in public restrooms and in public showers, and it has just alerted you of a potential threat. You look up—very up, not at all down—and you recognize his face.

Somehow, and you or anyone you know has never been able to explain how, this guy is always in the gym. He is never not there. You have come to the gym at all hours of the day, and he is ever-present, playing racquetball or hitting on the underage receptionist.

Rec specs, headband, wristbands, racquet in hand, waiting for challengers or enthusiastically smashing his way to victory, his grunts reverberating off of the hardwood and shaking the glass door.

He stands next to you now, wearing only his rec specs.

"You have dishonored me," he hisses.

"I don't know what you're talking about."

"You have shamed me," he says. "That court is my court, and you used it without my permission."

"I stopped at the desk, and they said that no one had reserved it..."

"That court is always my court. Everyone here knows that."

"Listen, dude, sorry about that, but maybe pencil yourself in next time?"

He punches the shower wall. "No! This transgression will not go unpunished," he yells. "I challenge you to a battle of fisticuffs, to be settled immediately!" He slaps you and raises his fists, awaiting your response.

You have had enough. One o-soto-gari, and he will never swing a racquet again. You reach forward to grip his collar and sleeve, but you discover an absence of fabric. He is naked, save for his foggy rec specs. Your years of training in the gi—grabbing lapels and sleeves and pant legs, perfecting loop chokes and toreando guard passes—were for naught. You had always assumed that gi fashion would catch on, that the world would disregard jeans and polos and adopt the comfort of a double-weave gi. You were wrong, and you are about to lose a challenge match to a guy wearing rec specs.

The explanation:

The Brazilian Jiu-Jitsu uniform, the gi, is a major point of contention. Advocates of the gi argue that the numerous grip points force a jiu-jiteiro to be more technical. With so many ways for him to be swept or submitted, his form and technique must be perfect. In the gi, when you make a mistake, the friction of the uniform and the control that grips provide make it impossible to simply rip out, which is often possible without the gi. Members of the anti-gi camp argue that training in the gi is not realistic, that since people do not wear gis and since MMA is not fought in the gi learning to control and attack with gi grips is pointless. And when you are faced with a real-life no-gi situation, your gi instincts will fail you in a big, painful way.

The gi versus no-gi debate rages in jiu-jitsu forums across the web and has been raging for years. I have no intention of continuing that battle here, but the notion that training in a gi is impractical for a hypothetical street fight needs to be addressed.

As far as self-defense is concerned, training in the gi is far more practical than training without it.

Our shower scenario aside, virtually every street fight encounter will involve both attackers wearing clothing of some sort. You can use this clothing to your advantage through grips, but more importantly, your opponent can use your clothing to his advantage, which is an oft-ignored point among gi haters. The first time someone jerks you around by your shirt is disorienting. The way it affects your balance and affects your mobility is strange. If this first encounter is in the midst of a fight, you are likely to find yourself eating a few punches while you determine the best solution to this alien problem.

After a few years of training in the gi, a collar grip is unsurprising, and you are accustomed to maintaining your composure even as you get yanked back and forth. Better yet, you can use your gi training to

Rec Spec Guy accosts Marshal in the shower, initiating a shoulder grab from behind. Marshal counters by turning toward Rec Spec Guy, looping his left arm around Rec Spec Guy's right arm, and locking his hands. Marshal then applies upward pressure with his hands to wrench Rec Spec Guy's right arm out of the socket, forever destroying the power of his backhand.

eliminate the grips, either by breaking them or by countering with grips of your own. If you do not train in the gi, you will never develop this level of grip awareness.

But what if you get in a fight at the beach? Or during a massage?

Or at a speedskating meet?

Underhooks and overhooks. Even if you have never trained no-gi, you are familiar with these tools, and you will have little trouble using them against an untrained attacker. Typically, a jiu-jiteiro that trains in the gi also trains without it, making him more prepared to deal with an unexpected street fight than someone who trains exclusively in no-gi.

And besides, training in the gi is fun. If you are really worried that your gi training will never be put to use, maybe you should start going to fancier parties where people wear more than work boots and cut-off jean shorts.

I Have a Gun and It Goes Pop Pop

The scenario:

You are at a family cookout. You manage to duck your crazy great aunt and your great grandmother, both of whom are convinced you are still eight years old, but are entangled in a conversation with your parents about your life and your career.

"When are you going to give up that writing stuff and get a real job?"

You shrug.

"Are you still fighting? Aren't you a little old for Karate?"

You stutter your way out, stepping backward with every syllable, and make your escape. You loop around the above ground pool—giving it a wide berth because your cousins are swimming and they are little shits— slip between the swing set and sandbox, and work your way into the conversation by the beer coolers. Your little brother brought his new girlfriend, and she is talking about guns with your redneck uncle. You casually listen, preferring a discussion of trigger setting and barrel bores to a discussion of your hopeless future and your unique ability to endlessly disappoint your parents.

The conversation continues. Your little brother's girlfriend and your redneck uncle talk about their love for the National Rifle Association (she has the same sticker on her convertible that he has on his farm-use-only pick-up truck), and they rattle off dozens of brand names and metric measurements. Then your little brother's girlfriend looks up and notices you sipping your wine cooler.

"I don't think we've met," she says.

Your little brother introduces you.

"Oh, you do Brazilian Jiu-Jitsu, right?" she asks.

You know that answering this question never ends well, but you nod nonetheless.

"I took a few self-defense classes," she says, "but then my dad bought me a handgun. There's no punch or kick that can beat a gun."

You take a long drink. "Well," you say, "Learning a martial art would still be useful just in case you can't get to your gun fast enough."

"What? You don't think I am fast enough?" She reaches into her purse and draws her gun, a pink Beretta. She cocks it and points it at you. "Was that fast enough for you? Huh? Huh?"

You drop your wine cooler, spilling the sweet purple nectar into the grass. You raise your hands and try to breathe.

"N-n-n-n-ow listen," you say. "I meant no offense. S-s-s-s-so we can put the gun down." You did not notice before, but now it's as clear as a sweat soaked pair of whitie tighties in a humid dressing room: she has crazy eyes. They bulge, tiny red veins flexing and rippling in the whites of her eyes as her forehead twitches. At a Rickson Gracie seminar you learned never to look into crazy eyes, but you are trapped, the vortex of her unpredictability sucking you into a world where the Kardashians win Nobel prizes and Bill O'Reilly is a journalist.

"Where's your fancy judo now, huh? Aren't you going to kick the gun out of my hand and flip me over? Huh? Huh? This is freedom. This is America. This is the only martial art I need. Made in America, not in Brazil!" Her hand shakes. The pink barrel blurs as it rocks in and out of your face.

"You're right. I'm sorry," you say. "Jiu-jitsu is silly. Kid stuff. You win."

She stares into your eyes, her face still twitching. Her forehead relaxes and she lowers the gun. "Good," she says, smiling. "I'm glad we worked that out. Anybody want a beer? I'm thirsty." She turns and bounces away, heading toward the coolers.

You look to your brother.

"Well," he starts, looking into his beer. "I don't think the break-up is going to go well."

The explanation:

Weapon defense, like multiple attacker defense, is an imperfect science. Theoretically, there is a best way to disarm a gun or a knife or a baseball bat or a chair or a swordfish, but none of these techniques are preferable to fleeing or to avoidance. If a weapon is involved, a sane martial artist assumes that they have already lost and looks for a way out, either through compliance—like handing over your fake leather wallet and the expired gym membership that it contains—or through retreat. This is the most reasonable course of action. Any martial artist that tells you disarming a weapon is easy, and I have met such individuals, is insane and should not be trusted.

Pulling a gun in a fight is like being that third grader that whips out the dynamite play in a game of rock, paper, scissors. It's super cheap, but you cannot deny who is the winner.

Is gun and knife defense part of the Gracie self-defense curriculum? Absolutely. If you are ever in a situation where you have no choice, knowing what to do is better than not knowing what to do. At that point in the curriculum, however, you should know that willingly engaging an attacker with a weapon is a dumb-shit move. By the time you start practicing knife defense, you have probably rolled with your instructor and the advanced students, all of whom mopped the mat with your carcass, like a shark dragging a baby seal to the depths of the ocean. Jiu-jiteiros know that fighting is hard, and they face this reality almost every day. They know how quickly a fight can end, and they know that the human body is far from invincible. They know that losing or getting hurt is far too easy, even when weapons are not involved.

Train for worst-case scenarios, but do not be an idiot.

The flipside of this issue is the argument that owning a gun negates the need to train Brazilian Jiu-Jitsu. This argument is often made for other quick-fix self-defense weapons, like cans of mace or stun guns or tasers. The belief is that these weapons are so powerful and easy to use that owning them immediately trumps anything that could be learned on the mat. Why spend all that time training and practicing chokes and escapes when you can point and shoot? There are a number of reasons actually.

If you draw a weapon, whether you are drawing a gun or a can of pepper spray, you escalate the situation to one of life or death. For this reason, police officers follow strict guidelines of what variables justify an increase in force. A drunk mouthing off and perhaps threatening violence does not justify the unholstering of a firearm. If that same drunk becomes violent, a baton or a taser may be necessary and justified. If that violence involves a weapon or some sort, then the use of a firearm is acceptable. The logic behind this behavior is that the choice of initiating violence greater than that of your opponent can actually make a situation worse. Civilians should take this to heart because they do not have the benefit of a belt loaded with gear, a partner in the passenger seat, and back-up a radio call away. If you point a gun at someone, you are telling them that you are prepared and willing to end their life, which will likely make them feel the same way about you even if they had no desire to kill you when the problem first began.

If a firearm is your only means of self-defense, you lack the ability to choose how a situation evolves. With your gun in your purse, in your waistband, or in your glove compartment, you are defenseless, so you are stuck choosing between having no means of protecting yourself or drawing your weapon and potentially ending someone's life. And remember, just as we discussed in the section on eye-gouging, you will have to later justify your use of force, which could be tricky if you just shot a guy in a bar fight.

If you do own a firearm for self or home-defense purposes, I have no problem with that, so do not misunderstand me. However, a gun is not a cure all, and treating it as such is a mistake for reasons beyond conflict escalation. First of all, too few people actually practice using the weapons that they carry. I have had many individuals, from friends to strangers, tell me that because they carry mace or a pistol that they feel safe. When I ask them how much training they have had in drawing, arming, and using their weapon of choice, they typically say very little or none, especially if they are packing pepper spray or a taser. For some reason, they believe that using a weapon is as simple as point and shoot.

Drawing a weapon from a concealed location can be challenging if you are under immense stress, and that same stress will also affect your ability to arm and discharge that weapon. Even at close quarters, hitting a moving target can be tough, especially if you are frantic and shaking and disoriented. If you are spraying mace or pepper spray, you should also consider the direction of the wind and be fully prepared for some of your weapon to blow back into your own face, even under perfect conditions. That's assuming, of course, you have the chance to fire in the first place.

A highly trained gun owner can draw and fire in seconds, but even firearm experts admit that this is sometimes too slow. If an attacker is within ten yards of you, the chances are high that he can close the distance before you can draw and fire. It seems silly because we always think of bullets as being crazy fast. They are, but hands can be slow and can make mistakes. In a scenario like this, where you are unable to use your weapon for one reason or another, you are prepared to continue defending yourself if you have trained Brazilian Jiu-Jitsu. Better yet, you are skilled at controlling and incapacitating, which will come in handy if your attacker is after your weapon. In the end, there is nothing wrong with owning a gun or a weapon for self-defense, but you should practice with that weapon frequently and you should train jiu-jitsu so that you are not helpless in situations where you do not have a weapon or where using a weapon is excessive.

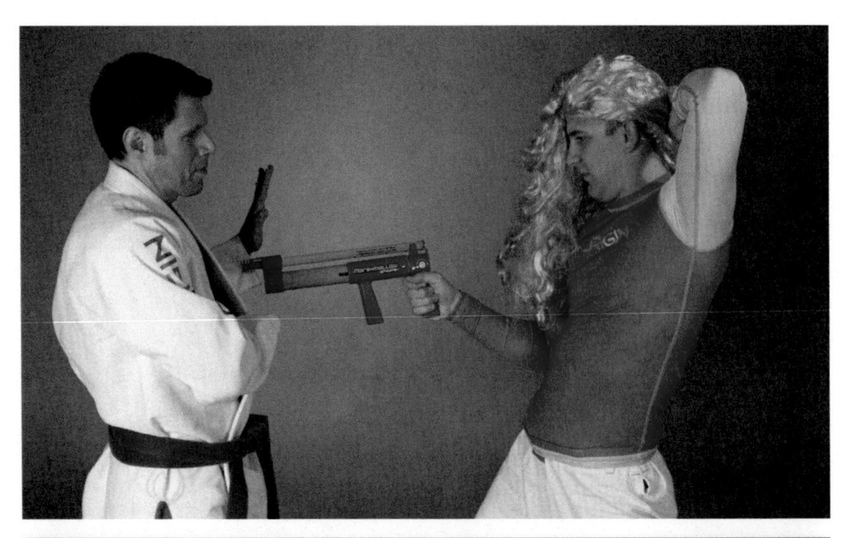

Previous: A striking blonde (or a time-traveling Brett Michaels, accounts vary) pulls a gun on Darryl and demands his dignity. Darryl side steps out of the line of fire and establishes double wrist control. From there, he applies armbar pressure to finish the fight.

Above: Darryl realizes that attempting to disarm a gun is far too risky and instead tries to deescalate the situation by giving the beautiful blonde his wallet.

Because It's Gay

The scenario:

You are over at a friend's house to watch a pay-per-view, and you are settling into your favorite spot on the couch. You have a plate of nachos in your lap, and your preferred adult beverage in your hand. You enjoy these nights. Your friends are your training partners, and an evening where you are not trying to break each others' arms is a welcome change of pace. And a guy is fighting another guy for the belt, and they totally hate each other and were jerks at the weigh-ins. That never happens, so this card should be unique and interesting.

Two nachos later and your one friend—you know the one, you love him even though he is a train wreck—rolls in, and to your surprise, he is joined by another friend. You are not optimistic about this man. His cheeks are oddly sunken, his gaze is shifty, and a strange odor wafts from his oversized t-shirt. He carries a brown paper bag and a shot glass.

You and your training partners watch as this individual sits down. He looks around but does not say anything or introduce himself. He removes a new bottle of tequila from the brown paper bag, breaks the seal, and pours himself a shot. And another. And another.

When the fights begin, a striking exchange quickly becomes a clinch with one fighter pressing the other against the cage.

"Awe man," the once silent Tequila Man shouts, "I hate this hugging shit. If a dude hugged me, man, I'd be so mad. Hugging isn't fighting!"

You look around. Three of your friends are lifetime wrestlers and another trains Muay Thai. They appear annoyed, but they, like all grapplers, have heard comments like this before. They continue watching.

After a few minutes and a few shots of tequila, the fight goes to the ground, which enrages Tequila Man. He shouts, "I am so sick of this gay shit. Fight! Don't hump each other!"

Again, your training partners, fully capable of stomping Tequila Man like they were playing their girlfriends at *Mario Kart*, do not respond. They look to each other, roll their eyes, and return their attention to the fights.

At the next intermission, Tequila Man staggers outside to smoke. Your host, one of the wrestlers in the room, gets up and locks the door.

"Listen, guys," he says. "We need to establish a dress code or a guest list or something. Maybe an entrance exam."

The explanation:

Homophobia is all-too common, and every jiu-jiteiro has been told that jiu-jitsu is "gay." We are told that guard is missionary, that north/south is 69, and that mount is cowgirl. We are told that rolling around on a mat with another man is nothing short of homosexual, and that no self-respecting straight 'merican would train a martial art like that. When you are a white belt and hear these comments, you become enraged, and you shout, and you defend your art. By the time you reach purple belt, you let out a sigh of disappointment and accept that your friendship with this person has ended.

As far as I know, there is no known cure for homophobia. Rumors and legend suggest that Carlos Gracie had developed such a cure after perfecting the Gracie Diet but later decided that someone afflicted with homophobia was unworthy of jiu-jitsu and thus unworthy of a cure. He gave the cure to a young boy, sending him up the Amazon river, deep into the jungle, where the cure could be hidden and guarded by an ancient Brazilian tribe. When the American Civil Liberties Union heard that the cure existed, they attempted to locate this tribe, but deforestation had driven them from their homes, and no one knows whether the cure was destroyed or whether it is lost in the Amazon.

Or so they say. For now, however, you can reasonably assume that your defense of jiu-jitsu will not sway their stiff beliefs. Save yourself the frustration and walk away.

That said, jiu-jitsu is not sexual, hetero or otherwise.

To say that jiu-jitsu is sexual is to suggest that all forms of physical contact are inherently sexual, and that is simply not true. We hug our family members, and cultures outside of 'merica aren't afraid to kiss their family members. We hold hands with our children, and we wrestle with our dogs. Physical contact does not have to be, and is often not, sexual. To suggest otherwise reveals a significant lack of maturity.

Grappling is one of the oldest sports in the world. In cultures across the globe, both ancient and contemporary, we have found variations of grappling, for sport and for combat. History suggests that grappling has existed for as long as humans have existed, which suggests that grappling is in our nature. It's ingrained in our species. Grappling is a part of being human, whether you do it with your brothers when your mom steps outside or whether you wrestle your way to a gold medal. Grappling is not going away.

Also, I am not so sure that the gay community appreciates the connection either. I once asked a gay friend of mine what he thought of people comparing jiu-jitsu to gay sex, and he said that it offended him.

"How would you feel if someone compared the way you make love to a bar fight? Wouldn't you be offended?"

I had never thought of it like that before. "Well," I said, "I am as graceful as a swan, so I don't think anyone would ever say that about me." "Yeah, right." I really am as graceful as a swan.

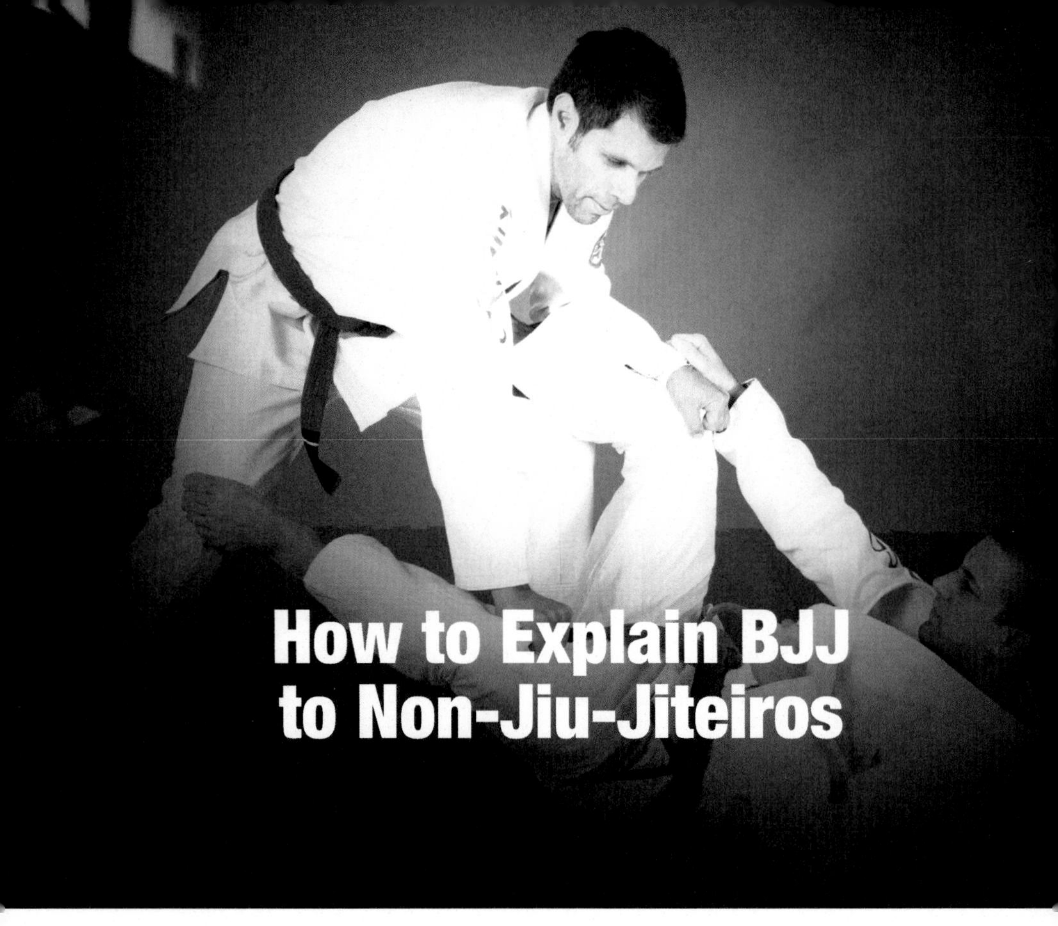

How to Explain BJJ to Non-Jiu-Jiteiros

STEP ONE

DON'T.

The Bean Dip Problem

If you insist on ignoring the previous advice, you are either brave or stupid. In either case, I do not want you to venture into danger alone. Having built my career in the fight industry, I have had to talk about jiu-jitsu on a daily basis. Your profession, somehow, is a major defining factor of who you are, so if someone has never met me they invariable ask, "What do you do?" And then I have to explain the premise behind my books and what working with professional fighters is like. Darryl, my coauthor, does not have this problem. He gets to smile and say that he is an entrepreneur and a designer, which makes him infinitely cooler and more interesting at parties. This is one of the many reasons I hate Darryl.

Anyway, to successfully define jiu-jitsu, you have to navigate a tumultuous ocean filled with World War II naval mines and zombie mermaids. The popularity of jiu-jitsu may be growing, but ignorance and misconceptions of our art abound. As an official jiu-jiteiro, with your awesome decoder ring and secret handshake, you know this all too well. You know that defining jiu-jitsu is problematic and that explaining a technique is much too handsy for any setting that does not involve loud music, flashing lights, and a fog machine, leaving you to rely entirely on words to convey the complex intersection of positioning, leverage, and strategy that is jiu-jitsu.

When you are forced to verbalize jiu-jitsu, you are actually facing a multi-layered challenge. Think of it like eating some amazing layered bean dip. The very bottom layer might be your favorite, but attempting to skip directly to the final layer will create an irreversible disaster of cheese and beans and salsa spilled all over your immaculate white carpet. You need a plan, a very specific technique for cutting through the many layers with a single tortilla chip, without spillage and without breakage. Explaining jiu-jitsu is no different. As badly as you want to skip to the end where a person either falls in love with jiu-jitsu or stops bothering you about it, you cannot. You have to deal with the layers.

The first three layers are fairly consistent, you must:

1. Identify the nature of and intention behind the jiu-jitsu questioning.

2. Explain that jiu-jitsu is not Tae Kwon Do.

3. Recite your favorite short explanation.

After those three layers, you must contend with three ever-present challenges, which are as follows:

4. Over sharing your passion for jiu-jitsu could give people the wrong idea.

5. Your family will never understand or accept jiu-jitsu.

6. Be careful not to become a Means-Well White Belt.

If you follow my initial advice and skip the bean dip problem altogether by simply choosing to avoid scenarios where you would have to explain jiu-jitsu, you will never have to navigate the murky depths of jiu-jitsu verbalization, and you will never have the feelings of gassy discomfort afterward. In the event that you are left with no choice, read this chapter carefully and heed my advice. This knowledge is the product of many failures to explain jiu-jitsu, resulting in countless awkward silences and hours of me sitting alone at the end of the bar nursing appletinis. Don't let that happen to you.

The 4 Kinds of Inquisitors

The first obstacle is the initial raising of the topic of jiu-jitsu. It can come in many forms and be propelled by various intentions, and you should adjust your strategy based upon the scenario, just as you would in a grappling match. Choose the wrong technique at the wrong time and you are getting your face smashed and your pride destroyed, metaphorically and perhaps literally depending on present company. In this section, you will find a breakdown of the four most common kind of inquisitors and suggestions for how to counter them. After you have drilled these techniques, you can begin to experiment with your own variations, reading and responding to social cues as they arise, but that level of verbal jiu-jitsu is incredibly advanced and can take years to develop. It will come with time, so pace yourself and master the basics. Here is what you should look out for and how you should handle it.

1. The Two-Pronged Question

The initial challenge of explaining Brazilian Jiu-Jitsu is that you are actually answering two separate questions at once. Not only are you trying to verbalize what Brazilian Jiu-Jitsu is and how it works, but you are also trying to verbalize why you train Brazilian Jiu-Jitsu. These are two very different yet equally complex issues, and if you start to answer the wrong question first, the person that you are talking to is likely to be confused. If he wanted an explanation of the mechanics and strategy of jiu-jitsu, going all Maya Angelou about the beauty and emotional satisfaction of jiu-jitsu will be a turn off. At the same time, if he was curious to know why you personally are interested in jiu-jitsu, blabbering on and on about leverage and positioning will not help you make your case.

Solution:

You: "Do you mean what is it, or why do I do it?"

2. The Bait

The Office Aikido Guys of the world will prod you about jiu-jitsu for the purpose of telling you how much better their martial art is compared to yours. They will attempt to disguise their intentions, but be on the lookout for a subtle smirk and a childlike gleam in their eyes. Their plan is to trick you into revealing your belief in jiu-jitsu's superiority so that they can argue, barraging you with many of the misconceptions that we covered in the previous chapter. This is a real life internet troll. The only way to convince a person like this that jiu-jitsu is indeed better than their combat ready kung fu yoga is to spar with them. Unfortunately, if you initiated a challenge match with every person that told you their martial art was better than jiu-jitsu, you would never have a day off from fighting, and you would be a douche. Don't be a douche. Be a well-rested jiu-jiteiro.

Solution:

You: "Those are interesting points, but agree to disagree. I think that Aqua Man is the greatest super hero of all time. What do you think of that?"

3. The Macho Posture

The only thing worse than a martial arts nerd arguing with you about the merits of jiu-jitsu, which is kind of like arguing with your weird cousin that eats paint chips and has giant posters of anime babes in his bathroom, is a meathead that wants to compare his bench press record to your scissor sweep. This guy brings up jiu-jitsu to embarrass you. He knows that his muscles are bigger than yours, and he needs to belittle others to feel even bigger. This is another situation where there is no point in taking offense to insults or to challenges. The days of challenge matches are over. Jiu-jitsu has proven itself, and you should not feel obligated to throw down with every juicer that tries to get a reaction from you. Use verbal jiu-jitsu instead.

Solution:

You: "How much do you bench press? Yeah, my high score on Pac Man is close to that. Any tips for increasing my numbers like you have?"

4. Polite Fake Interest

Talking to strangers is more than dangerous; it's awkward. Silence to most is more horrifying than a staph infection, and they will do anything to fill a lull in conversation. This is why people talk about drivel like the weather or politics, and it's why jiu-jitsu is the best place to make friends. Not only do you have a constant source of interesting material—because nothing is more interesting than jiu-jitsu—but when you get bored you can fight each other. Resuscitating a dying conversation with a non-jiteiro is not easy, and do not be surprised if they feign interest in jiu-jitsu to keep noise in the air. By now, your girlfriend has probably told you that you talk about jiu-jitsu too much, so if your girlfriend is uninterested, do not torture an acquaintance. Change the subject.

Solution:

You: "Yeah, jiu-jitsu is a good time. Did you see the last episode of the Kardashians? Scott Disick is the man."

I should clarify the source of my Kardashian knowledge. When a friend introduced me to AMC's *the Walking Dead,* the second season was about to begin. Since I was (and am) in a committed long-term relationship, television viewing was an act of compromise. To convince my significant other to watch *the Walking Dead* with me, I had to agree to watch the *Kardashians*, which aired immediately after. For me, it was like going from one zombie show to another. I care very little for fashion, celebrity gossip, or for reality television, and I had never watched any of the previous *Kardashian* shows. But then Scott Disick stepped into the frame.

If you are not familiar with Disick, you should be. Disick is the permanent boy toy of Kourtney Kardashian, the most attractive Kardashian sister. In what is usually an uneventful show, Disick displays black belt level verbal jiu-jitsu in his navigation of the increasingly complex Kardashian obstacle course. He zips through his days wearing classy suits and espousing poignant one liners, his self-satisfactory grin never wavering. He dabbles in this, and he dabbles in that, and he struts about with a level of self-confidence that jiu-jiteiro's could learn from, especially when talking to non-jiu-jiteiros. If someone does not understand the latest Disick development, he just flashes a smile, quips, and carries on. Haters aren't worth his time, and they should not be worth our time either.

No, BJJ is not Tae Kwon Do

Brazilian Jiu-Jitsu is not Tae Kwon Do. I feel I have to emphasize this point because I suspect that you have already bought ten copies of this book to give to the non-jiu-jiteiros in your life, and they need to hear this. Brazilian Jiu-Jitsu is definitely not Tae Kwon Do. I looked into it, so I can say this with 100 percent certainty.

The biggest clue that Brazilian Jiu-Jitsu is not Tae Kwon Do is that Tae Kwon do originated in Korea and is the national sport of South Korea, at least for now. *Starcraft,* however, may soon become the national sport, if my inability to be competitive in any online game is an indication of South Korean trends. For the time being, Tae Kwon Do is very much Korean and very much not Brazilian. See the provided map to gaze upon the geographic difference between Brazil and the Koreas yourself. As the graphic illustrates, the difference is significant.

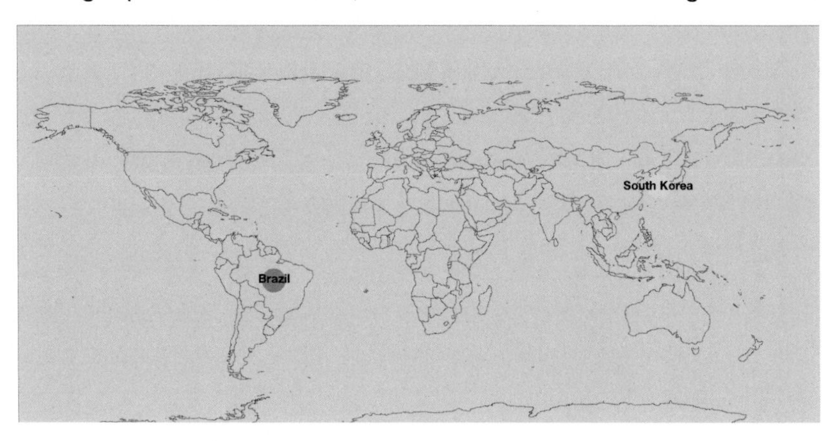

Yet, a soccer mom will hear that you train jiu-jitsu and say, "Oh yeah, my ten year old is a black belt in Tae Kwon Do too." It never fails.

Beyond the difference in geographic and cultural origins, jiu-jitsu and Tae Kwon Do differ in style and in practice. If you stumble upon a street fight between a jiu-jiteiro and a Kwon, for example, spotting the Kwon should be easy. You could analyze the style of the punches being thrown, or critique the crispness of the kicks, or compare the differences in footwork. A Kwon will bounce and dance, his combination of punches and kicks an aerial ballet of strikes. A jiu-jiteiro is more patient, more reserved. He will gauge the fluctuation of distance, observing the expansion and closure of space as his opponent attempts to launch an attack, looking for an opportunity to shoot or clinch. Where the Kwon's stance will be open, his hands rising and falling as he bobs and weaves and threatens kicks, the jiu-jiteiro will keep his hands up and his chin tucked, a tight defensive position.

And their haircuts will differ as well. For some reason, Kwon's love hair gel, so watch for glistening spikes and swoops. A jiu-jiteiro will likely have his hair cut short or shaved. If you consider all of these variables, you should be able to identify who practices what style.

Or you could wait 15 seconds and see who gets choked first. The Kwon always gets choked.

In Brazil, they calibrate stopwatches by the Kwon time standard. One Kwon equals 15 seconds, the time it takes for a jiu-jiteiro to submit a Tae Kwon Do expert. How long does it take you to paddle out to catch a wave? Probably about 12 Kwons. What took you so long? You are 50 Kwons late. These sorts of expressions are used constantly in Brazil, and as more and more Brazilians teach and compete in the United States, "hold on a Kwon" will become as commonplace as "hold on a second." The Kwon time standard is so precise—more accurate than the atomic clock—that Kwon calibrated stopwatches are the most accurate stopwatches ever made, which is why the most expensive and most desirable stopwatches are manufactured in Brazil.

Stylistic differences aside, training practices vary as well. Jiu-jitsu schools are scattered across the world and are usually found in any significantly populated area. Tae Kwon Do schools, on the other hand, are located exclusively next to home improvement stores like Lowes or Home Depot. Board breaking requires a great deal of lumber. Any distance between a Tae Kwon Do school and a lumber supply slows training significantly. Kwon instructors often negotiate agreements with home improvement chains where the home improvement chains supply the lumber free of charge, provided that the Kwon instructors use their child armies to cut the lumber to size, saving billions of dollars a year.

You will find no such use of child labor at Brazilian Jiu-Jitsu schools because we never break boards. If we were members of Saruman's army and the Ents were attacking, snapping wooden planks might be useful in a self-defense context, but we are not, so we have put our lumber combat skills on hold indefinitely. At least until Middle Earth is plunged into another bitter war, that is.

The last two differentiators are katas and children with black belts. In a jiu-jitsu school, you will not see either. We drill movements in isolation, by ourselves and with partners, but you will never see us rehearsing a dozen different solo dances, unless of course we are at the bar, have had too much to drink, and are not doing so well with the ladies. Kata, to us, is impractical. Awarding a black belt to a child that cannot vote, drive, or drink—legally at least—is also impractical. As my friend Jay Penn, not to be confused with his younger brother B.J. Penn, once put it: "You should not be able to abduct a black belt." A black belt that cries when you steal his Pokémon cards is an embarrassment to the art, which is why myself and 12 year olds will never have black belts in Brazilian Jiu-Jitsu.

Do not spend more than 10 Kwons explaining these differences to a non-jiu-jiteiro. Your time is better spent training.

Jiu-Jitsu is Kind of Like Wrestling But Not

In the rare case that you meet a person that is genuinely interested in jiu-jitsu, you should be able to explain jiu-jitsu in simple terms. To capitalize on the opportunity to convert an unbeliever, start with a one sentence description. My favorite line is:

"Jiu-jitsu is kind of like wrestling, except that we win by applying a submission hold instead of a pin, and we focus less on athleticism and more on techniques that will help a small guy defend himself against a big guy."

That's how I do it, but every grappler handles this challenge differently.

A True Story of Workplace Discrimination

When I moved back to Pittsburgh from Las Vegas, I continued freelance writing while I poked around for a fulltime job. With hundreds of published articles, four books, and a wealth of in-the-trenches marketing experience, I assumed that finding a position with reasonable pay would not be difficult. I was wrong, of course, but I eventually networked my way into a gig where I wrote meaningless brochures and developed extensive promotional campaigns.

After a few months at my makeshift desk in the corner, which doubled as the breakroom table, so I was forever brushing away crumbs and wiping-up sticky spots of unknown origins, my coworkers casually mentioned that they were glad they did not let my reputation scare them away.

"What do you mean?" I asked.

"All the fighting stuff. Choking people, cages. That's kind of sociopathic, you know?" one of the females responded.

"Is she serious?" I asked my boss, who was sitting nearby.

He laughed. "Well, yeah. You don't want someone violent and unpredictable in the office," he said. "It could be dangerous."

And they were serious. They had visited my website, read some articles, and browsed the sample chapters of my book. They assumed that since the fighting world was such a large part of my life that I was no different from an Affliction-wearing bar brawler. To them, jiu-jitsu was synonymous with street fighting, and someone who street fights is clearly not the kind of person that you want next to you at the office. Had I not called in a favor and had a friend put in a good word for me, I would have never even gotten the interview.

Even though this conversation occurred some time ago, it devastated me. I consider myself a friendly person, a good person. To be told that I was a suspected of going Unabomber on my coworkers hurt.

And shut up. I get beat up for a living. I am allowed to be sensitive on occasion.

People like this are everywhere. They fear what they do not understand, and too many people on the mixed martial arts side of the world overplay the fighter image, to the point that they resemble the same types of people we train to defend ourselves from. Jiu-jiteiros are lumped into this category all too-often simply by being associated with a facet of cage fighting. When you reveal that you train jiu-jitsu, the people around you may make this unfair generalization before you have the chance to deliver your personal variation of the It's Like Wrestling, But Not Speech. If you find yourself among people that may be prone to prescribing stereotypes, it may be wise to choose how you share your hobby carefully. You could end up on the wrong side of jiu-jitsu discrimination and miss out on the chance to take care of you or your family.

Darryl and I have contacted multiple human rights groups to inform them of these injustices, but they have yet to officially review our case. We are being diligent though. We will be heard, and the constitution will be amended to make jiu-jiteiro discrimination a crime.

This is one of the most pressing issues of our generation, and our choice to act or stand by and let these horrors against humanity continue will define how history views us for eternity.

Your Family Will Never Take BJJ Seriously

Unless your dad is the one that inspired or pushed you to start training, chances are that your family does not understand jiu-jitsu and thinks that you are pretty weird for wanting to roll around on a mat with sweaty people in pajamas. I am not a world champion grappler or a mega best-selling author, but jiu-jitsu gave me the opportunity to make an honest living doing and writing about an exciting, interesting sport. This is no secret, and my passion for jiu-jitsu is not a secret either. Anyone that has met me knows how important training is to me, and this includes my family.

Regardless, my parents ask, at least six times a year, "When will you give up that jiu-jitsu stuff?"

If they hear that I was injured training—which is often because my body is more fragile than an anorexic's self-esteem—they immediately push me to hang up my belt and take up a safer hobby instead, like golf or falconry. These are the same parents that signed me up to do rodeo when I was still rocking braces and avoiding cooties.

Yes, I did rodeo, and I did it often. Most of my participation was limited to what was called "drill team," which is like synchronized swimming but with horses. A drill team is comprised of ten to twenty riders and horses, all carrying flags. The team performs to music, executing a variety of maneuvers and feats to mark the beginning of an event or to fill an intermission slot. We even wore the same outfits, a Garth Brooks style black button-up with flames. If you think this sounds cool, you are a crazy person. It was incredibly lame, and for many years I refused to admit that my rodeo days ever happened. I never told anyone about drillteam, or calf-roping, or steer-wrestling, or that one time that I rode a bull.

For real, I rode a bull.

I was 13 years old, and after strapping myself into a chest protector and a full-face helmet, they dropped me down into the chute, a narrow pen with tall steel fencing, with a real bull. It was not a pro-circuit bull, but it was still a full-sized adult with a piece of rawhide strapped over the part of the bull that makes it a man. If you have ever had someone pull the tail of your belt between your legs to get a sweep, I imagine it feels like that except worse, as if someone was loop-choking your scrotum. This is why bulls buck the way they do, and this is also why they tend to run down riders or clowns in the arena. You would be just as angry if someone loop choked your balls.

You are probably thinking that since I am so strapped with powerful t-shirt fraying muscles that riding a bull would be easy for me. Unfortunately, at 100 pounds, my Super Nintendo trained fingers were not prepared for the brewing rage of the beast beneath me. I sat on its back. The bull shifted nervously. It's heaving ribs pressed my legs into the fence on either side, and it kicked nervously at a botfly, slamming a hoof against the gate. My full-face helmet smelled of manure, and an old football mouth guard covered in dirt and dried saliva dangled near my chin.

"You can use the mouth guard if you want," a rodeo clown said, leaning into the chute to get my attention.

I looked into his brightly colored face. My breath and my voice echoed in my helmet as I said, "No, thank you."

I wrapped the rawhide strap around my right hand and lifted my left hand into the air. I nodded that I was ready.

The gate swung open and the bull whirled into the open arena. His body heaved, flexing every sinew as it dipped its head forward and kicked its back legs out. The raw force that this creature could generate shocked me. I had been riding horses for years and had grown accustomed to balancing and gripping my way through bucks and rears. Compared to the buck of a bull, the buck of a horse is like riding stationary race car outside of K-Mart, leaving me sorely unprepared for my present task.

In bull riding, the goal is to stay on the bull for eight seconds. I lasted approximately zero seconds. That first bounce launched me off of the bull and across the arena, planting my face into the dirt and sand. A rodeo clown grabbed the back of my shirt and drug me to the fence as I struggled to poke my fingers through the mesh to dig the dirt out of my eyes.

And my mom and dad were in the stands, clapping, cheering, and laughing, the same parents that now often tell me that jiu-jitsu is too dangerous and that I should quit. For the most part, the rest of my family feels the same way, but they are not nearly as vocal.

Girlfriends too are trouble. If you start dating someone after you make the choice to commit to jiu-jitsu, convincing them that jiu-jitsu is a worthwhile, respectable endeavor will be slightly easier than if you start jiu-jitsu a few years into a long term relationship. In either case, jiu-jitsu can create problems, but accepting a time-sink that is already present is much easier than accepting a new one, for a girlfriend at least.

Relationships require time and effort. Jiu-jitsu requires time and effort. Your fulltime job requires time and effort. You only have so much time and effort, and a significant other will often find it difficult to accept your choosing open mat over a date night. Even after you explain how important jiu-jitsu is to you, how it mellows you out, how it keeps you healthy, and how it motivates you to be a better person, she will likely still feel slighted when jiu-jitsu comes first.

You can ease this conflict by balancing your life, making your significant other feel important while sneaking in as much training as you can, but the battle may never end until you find someone that understands, that gets the need to train. These people are special, and they are rare. If you find one, do not screw up. Give up a few training sessions here and there to keep the peace, and train your ass off when she goes out of town.

As for the rest of your family, pay no mind. They are probably as passionate about something as you are about jiu-jitsu, whether that passion is drinking beer, collecting stamps, or How It's Made reruns. You may not understand why your family members gravitate toward their hobbies, but you are decent enough not to constantly chide them for picking pastimes nowhere near as awesome as jiu-jitsu.

Nothing is as awesome as jiu-jitsu, and only families with the last name of Gracie will consistently agree with that.

The Means-Well White Belt

White belts are special people. They are enthusiastic about their recent discovery of jiu-jitsu, and their newfound passion is so exciting that they want to tell everyone, absolutely everyone, about jiu-jitsu. They watch every YouTube video, order every pay-per-view, and buy every instructional on the market, from the well-known to the incredibly obscure. They train every day, and their eagerness to learn has them asking dozens of questions and debating techniques.

This is awesome, and it's why I love white belts. I was like this once, and most of us probably were, but a white belt often stumbles into a bit of a dilemma. A white belt is likely the first of a social circle, or an isolated segment of a social circle, to start training jiu-jitsu. Suddenly, the sparkling new white belt is also a jiu-jitsu ambassador. His friends, knowing even less about the gentle art, ask him what are often very challenging questions, especially when watching a mixed martial arts bout or when comparing jiu-jitsu to another martial art.

These friends want to know why jiu-jiteiros make certain decisions in a fight, why they do one thing instead of another, and what they would do in a certain scenario. Questions like this can be difficult to answer, even for a purple or brown belt, but the new white belt feels as if he should know, as if he should be able to answer every question that is posed to him after three months of taking classes. The white belt does his best, fielding question after question and dumping book after book and video after video into his brain so that he can feel as though he has all of the answers. After a few weeks of pretending to have all of the answers, he starts to believe that he does. He has learned so much and seen so much, surely he has it figured out.

He means-well, he really does, but he mistakenly spreads misinformation about the art. He may fail to explain the purpose of a particular technique or approach. He may demonstrate a technique incorrectly. A number of scenarios are possible, and they all end with the white belt mistakenly getting it wrong. For the person he is talking to, a misunderstanding of technique or of theory can leave a poor impression of jiu-jitsu, which can make the typical non-jiteiro problems even worse. They may have sincerely been interested in jiu-jitsu at one point, but a poor experience with a neophyte tainted that interest forever, and they go on to believe in a silly martial art like aikido or iron crotch kung fu.

My confession: I was one of the worst means-well white belts that ever existed. When I first began training, few training options were available, so I began training in my backyard. Even after I found a school—not a very good one, I should add—no training facilities were anywhere near my university, so I along with a few friends started a grappling club. Of our group, I had the most experience, so I started teaching classes. After three months of training in my backyard and four months of training at a poorly-run gym, I was teaching other people how to grapple. Now, after training for some time at a legitimate school, I estimate that those initial seven months of training were equivalent to one month of training at what is now my home gym.

I was a leader. I was a jiu-jitsu missionary. I had the books. I had the DVDs. I felt that I was prepared to spread the word about jiu-jitsu, so I talked about it all the time. I demonstrated moves at parties. I invited friends to train. I explained the nuances of position and control during fights.

And I was almost entirely full of shit.

Despite my good intentions, my attempt at having all of the answers may have discouraged someone from training jiu-jitsu. I may have discredited the art. I may have taught bad techniques. Actually, I most certainly taught dozens of bad techniques.

No one ever told me that I did not have to have all of the answers. No one ever told me that I could say "I am not sure" or "I don't know; I'm pretty new."

Now, as an upper belt, I try to impart this wisdom to the new white belts at my school. I reassure them that it's okay to be new, that it's perfectly fine if they do not have all the answers.

White belts need to know that they are not expected to know everything, and upper belts should encourage white belts to readily admit this fact. By doing this, we can create a more positive image for jiu-jitsu, and white belts will know that it is better to seek out the answer than to pretend.

Street Ready Jiu-Jitsu

Life outside of the gym is hard. In the gym, the floors and walls are padded. Your favorite music is always playing. And your gi feels like a suit of liberally fabric-softened armor. Your place in the pecking order is clear, and even then your superiors are kind and push you to be a better person. As long as you are respectful of your training partners, you are welcomed and accepted into the community. You exercise. You learn. And you socialize. The mat is a comforting, welcoming place.

If there is one thing that growing up in a Pentecostal Christian private school taught me, it's that the streets are a brutal world ruled by chaos and evil, where everyone will attempt to force you to do hard drugs and encourage you to worship the devil. When you let your guard down on the street, your life will spiral into sin and then you will die a slow and painful dead. Many would argue that Jesus is your best protection, and we will not debate religion here, but a little known fact about Jesus is that he practiced an early form of Brazilian Jiu-Jitsu. The geopolitical chronology may seem to contradict that possibility, but scripture says that Jesus is, always has been, and always will be, so he could very easily have trained with the early founders of Brazilian Jiu-Jitsu while he was proselytizing in the middle east. All-powerful deities can do that.

In the book of Luke, Jesus says, "Train easy, my friends" when talking to his apostles. And some scholars believe that Jesus brought jiu-jitsu to heaven and taught it to the angels, which is why an angel was able to out-grapple Jacob in the book of Genesis for an entire day.

As a humble mortal, do whatever you can to survive the realities of the streets, and a large part of that preparation should be Brazilian Jiu-Jitsu. Without jiu-jitsu, you are doomed.

A great deal has been written about jiu-jitsu for self-defense and jiu-jitsu for the street. Many Brazilians have produced DVDs and written books on the subject. They demonstrate how to defend against knives, guns, litter, and multiple attackers. They talk about the differences between mat strategy and street strategy. They talk about how the use of certain techniques and positions changes when used on concrete instead of mats. And they pose against cinderblock walls, looking angry and wearing dark sunglasses.

Rather than rehash what has already been written—mostly because I do not look good in sunglasses—we are going to cover some unaddressed but all-too common street scenarios. You need to perfect all aspects of your street jiu-jitsu, so pay close attention to this chapter. You will use many of these techniques on a daily basis, and they just might save your life.

Wearing Gi Hickeys with Style and Panache

As a jiu-jiteiro, certain events are inevitable. If you train long enough, you will eventually submit your partners, you will bleed, you will earn your blue belt, and you will get at least one gi hickey. In truth, you will probably sport hundreds of gi hickeys in your jiu-jitsu career, and you will be forced to explain those hickeys to your friends, coworkers, and significant other.

A gi hickey, if you do not know, is a bruise or brush burn on your neck that you get during a training session. Gi hickeys are most commonly caused by lapel chokes, but they can also come from an aggressive lapel grip or a particularly rough arm choke. Abrasive fabric rubs the skin repeatedly, leaving behind a faint redness that unfortunately resembles the same sort of mark that eighth graders give each other in dark movie theaters. Beyond copious amounts of fabric softener, little can be done to prevent gi hickeys. Should a gi company discover anti-gi-hickey technology, they will make hundreds of dollars and may be able to purchase every gi manufacturer in Pakistan. Until then, you need to know how to cope with the socially awkward consequences of having gi hickeys all over your neck.

1. Your Significant Other

When you come home after a late night of jiu-jitsu, carrying the stench of six or seven training partners, crawling into bed and having to explain the marks on your neck can be uncomfortable. Your first line of defense is to not be a cheating douche bag and to keep that jiu-jiteiro charm leashed so that you are not known as a flirt. If you are nothing but a loyal spouse or boyfriend or girlfriend, you can avoid having to argue that the marks on your neck are from a sweaty dude that had no desire to sleep with you and not from that harlot at your office that always buys you coffee. You know the one. If you are loyal to your significant other and have no history of shadiness but still feel as though the gi hickey may create a discussion, mention that you drilled clock chokes all night and that your neck is terribly sore. Since your training habits are probably not a secret, this should eliminate any tinder and prevent a full-blown inferno.

2. At Work

Even though you have done your best to avoid discussing grappling with your non-jiteiro coworkers, the secret is likely out. As long as you maintain the overall cleanliness and professionalism of your image, and avoid having a Tyler Durden "Is that your blood?" exchange, a gi hickey should go unnoticed. In the event that it is noticed, a coworker will likely choose not to mention it. Most will assume that your gi hickey is just another minor training-related injury. They may still think that you are a weirdo for training jiu-jitsu, but the chances of it being mentioned are slim. In the event that the oddness of your training injuries is mentioned, shrug and carry on with trudging through the work day. If anyone ridicules you for your gi hickey, smile, and say, "I'm just trying to stay active. It's so easy to put on weight when you work at an office all day." Glance down at their stomach, look back up, smile a little wider, and shrimp back to your cubicle.

3. In Public

When you are out and about among complete strangers (civilians) wear your gi hickeys with pride. A gi hickey is not all that different from a black eye. You trained hard, and the rough and tumble nature of our sport left something for you to remember it by. To onlookers, however, a visible training injury can take on many meanings. A black eye, for example, can mean one of two things: you won a fight but got hit once, or you got hit once and lost the fight embarrassingly fast. You can remove any doubt of your fighting ability by maintaining a confident jiu-jiteiro strut. When an onlooker notices your gi hickeys, they will think only one thought: "damn, someone has been sucking on that neck like an owl going after a Tootsie Pop."

They will never consider the possibility of a lapel choke. Ever. So go ahead and strut your way through that one too. Except if you are with your mom. Because if you are standing next to your mom with gi hickeys and a confident strut... well, that would be weird. It's your mom.

4. In the Gym

Put on your gi and earn a few more. Anyone that is devoted to the mat is bruised and scraped and sore. Something so commonplace need not be discussed. Focus instead on what's important: beat the crap out of that head squeezer, and hone your technique in the process.

How to Break a Crazy Girlfriend's Guard

Conventional jiu-jitsu wisdom says not to wash your belt. In some superstitious way, the grime of your belt locks in your hard work and your experience. The dirt is a symbol of where you have been and speaks to where you are going. A tattered and frayed belt can be a beautiful artifact, but two scenarios are cause for washing your belt thoroughly and immediately. The first: a staph outbreak. A staph infection is not to be trifled with, and even the most superstitious jiu-jiteiros agree that washing away the magic stored within a belt is a necessary sacrifice under these circumstances. A staph infection could ruin your career or the career of one of your teammates. For the good of the team, of the brotherhood, we lay down our belts together, and scrub the hell out of everything in sight.

If you have ever seen or had a staph infection, you understand why jiu-jiteiros take sanitation seriously. If you are unfamiliar with staph infections, put this book down and go make a big pot of spaghetti with chunky tomato sauce. Heap the noodles and sauce into a bowl, and forgo the fork. Instead, grab the special noodle spoon, the wooden one with the tines all around the perimeter of the spooning area like a super spork. Settle into your office chair and enjoy a few mouthfuls of your meal. Savor the texture of the noodles and the sweetness of the sauce, that delicate interplay of basil and tomato highlighted by a dusting of parmesan.

Then, Google "Kevin Randleman staph."

Congratulations. You will never again eat spaghetti.

In one of my previous books, I asserted that love is like a staph infection, and my fiancée demands that I revise that statement. Crazy girlfriend love is like a staph infection, which is why you should never stick your belt in crazy. If you do, wash it immediately and thoroughly with a powerful disinfectant. Failing to cleanse your belt of crazy could cause the disease to spread to your friends and family, poisoning everyone and everything that you hold dear. Even your dog is in danger. This is the second scenario where washing your belt as acceptable, and none of your training partners will hold it against you.

Again, disaster can be averted if you heed the advice of the many generations of men and women that have come before you, so I repeat: never stick your belt in crazy.

But sometimes crazy girlfriends are adept at disguising their intentions. They lull you into passivity and pull you into their guard. They continue an easy roll, lazily locking a closed guard and lightly gripping your sleeves. You play along, enjoying the friendly match. You believe that she is just being quirky, a giddy sort of high energy flirting. For a moment, you think that this could be love. The buzzer sounds, but her guard does not open. It closes tighter. She grips your lapel, digging for a deep cross collar grip. Her legs climb up your shoulders and lock a high guard. You try to explain that the match is over, that the buzzer rang, but her face has changed. She smiles, and her eyes morph into bottomless pits of despair and clinginess.

You are trapped. Her guard is tight, and her clutches slink deeper and deeper with every passing second. Your belt is now stuck in crazy, and you have to break the guard and escape before you can rinse away the filth.

Jiu-jitsu theory tells us that the key to escaping a bad position is prevention. Maintain proper posture, and do not give your opponent an opening to exploit by remaining technical and composed. Anticipate attacks. Defend early.

But how do you predict crazy? What are the warning signs?

The Super Secret Brazilian Jiu-Jitsu Research Center, which we discussed in the first chapter, has been working on this problem for decades. The team at the SSBJJRC, which carries on the tradition of Brazilian Jiu-Jitsu organizations relying upon inconvenient acronyms (I'm looking at you, IBJJF), has invested over four billion dollars and lost 42 lives in the pursuit of a foolproof crazy girlfriend prevention system. This is the same team that spearheaded bully prevention research and the underrated mounted ostrich hand-to-hand combat system, which received brief critical acclaim in Australia. As of the print date of this book, the crazy girlfriend prevention system, codenamed "Operation War Pig," is far from complete.

My source within the SSBJJRC says that the project is stalled on preliminary detection. The most advanced forms of crazy are capable of remaining hidden for weeks in many cases and for years in the worst cases. Crazy girlfriends are SR-71s. You do not know they are near until your mountain hamlet is in flames.

As text messaging rose to prominence, the SSBJJRC abandoned handwriting analysis and began to analyze text messaging style and word choice, looking for a pattern, a tell, a tried-and-true sign that your belt is about to touch crazy. Emoticons seemed promising, and the research team zeroed in on the winky face over all others. The following is a paragraph from a leaked SSBJJRC research document:

> **Our analysis of 32 million text messages finds that the winky face is the most emotionally loaded and incorrectly-interpreted emoticon**

that has ever been invented. We conclude that a winky face can have one of four meanings:

1. **"LOL, I'm not sure how to end this message so I will just put a winky face because it's friendly and positive, LOL."**
2. **"I think I am being friendly and playful but do not realize how awkward I am."**
3. **"I will call you 40 times in an hour and burn your gis in my driveway to prove my love."**
4. "Drop everything, find me, and sleep with me right now."

These findings are the closest we have come to a reliable detection protocol. However, we recommend exploring a new research direction as preliminary studies reveal that single males, in all circumstances without fail, assume that a winky face represents the fourth meaning, nullifying any possible detection protocol. We are therefore shifting our focus to analyzing Pinterest boards and pinning habits.

Though a reliable detection technique remains a dream, you should still practice environmental scanning and avoid potential ambush points. If you do encounter a crazy girlfriend, do not make any sudden movements. Maintain as much distance as you can, back away slowly without exposing your back, and run.

For the white belt guard breakers out there, here is a list of places where you should be on high alert:

- Sorority formals.
- Your distant cousin's wedding.
- West Virginia strip clubs.
- Websites dedicated to Christian singles.

- The local courthouse.
- WalMart.
- Cleveland.

In the event that you find yourself trapped in a crazy girlfriend's guard, and you will know when it happens (hint: your friends will tell you that your girlfriend is crazy three months before you admit it to yourself), you must not hesitate. You must keep your wits about you and execute a technical escape to free yourself from this incredibly dangerous position.

1. Take a deep breath and mentally prepare yourself for the battle ahead. Inform a close friend that you are about to step into harm's way, and make him or her vow to keep you on course.
2. Calmly explain to your crazy girlfriend that the relationship has come to an end and that you wish her the best. Then run.
3. Lock your doors and your windows.
4. Set your email to automatically forward all correspondences from the crazy girlfriend to the trash folder.
5. Delete her phone number.
6. Do not call her.
7. Do not succumb to the booty call.
8. Seriously, do not call her.
9. Train. Jiu-jitsu is the ultimate cure. If it ever starts to hurt, go to the mat and train it out.

In the event that you are dealing with a black belt crazy girlfriend guard, skip to step ten:

10. Lawyer up.

Good luck. Hopefully you succeed where many men have fallen.

Your Love Life and Jiu-Jitsu

Two things in life are demanding of your time: jiu-jitsu and your significant other. Oftentimes, date night will conflict with class times. Your girlfriend's best friend's wedding will invariably fall on the same day of a big tournament. And that seminar that you have been looking forward to for months will conflict with your girlfriend's birthday, and you will not recognize this conflict until you are pulling your gi out of the drier and she jokingly comments, "Why are you doing laundry? You won't need your gi for dinner tonight."

Balancing jiu-jitsu and romantic relationships is challenging. We have all been there, and I have had three relationships end with the following exchange:

"If you had to pick between me or jiu-jitsu, which would you choose?"

"Yeah… I'll just leave for the gym now…"

Jiu-jitsu is like a relationship. You must dedicate time and effort to making it better. You will have good days, and you will have bad days. If you keep putting in positive energy, you will get progress back out. On the same token, relationships are like jiu-jitsu. Sometimes you are on top, and sometimes you are on bottom. Sometimes you win a fight, and sometimes you lose a fight. There are ups and downs, but if you approach the relationship with maturity and with dedication, the rewards are great and far outweigh any of the bumps that you will encounter along the way.

If you intend to strive for jiu-jitsu perfection for the rest of your life while also having a happy, healthy relationship with a significant other, you must find a way to satisfy both desires.

Here are three tips for being a devoted jiu-jiteiro and a devoted partner:

1. Don't Be Like Marcelo Garcia

Marcelo Garcia is a phenomenal grappler. And so is B.J. Penn. And Dave Camarillo. And Demian Maia. And John Danaher. And Renzo Gracie (and pretty much every Gracie for the matter). We look up to these grapplers, and we seek to emulate their often god-like abilities, but there is one thing that all of these individuals have in common that the vast majority of us normal guys and girls do not: they have a lot of time to train.

Marcelo began training as a young teen and was able to dedicate upwards of eight hours a day, five to six days a week, to training. B.J. started somewhat later in life, but in the three years between his white belt and his black belt, B.J. had the resources to do nothing but train. All day. Every day. If Marcelo and B.J. trained 40 hours a week, five eight hour days, it would take an average jiu-jiteiro, one that has a full time job and a family, that trains three times a week for two hours a session roughly six and a half weeks to accumulate the amount of mat time that Marcelo and B.J. get in a week. Let me repeat that: six and half weeks to do what elite level grapplers accomplish in one week. Play that same distribution out over a year, and the result is a monumental disparity in training time.

This is an important point to consider when evaluating our own progress and how we budget our time. To aspire to be as talented as elite level grapplers (like Marcelo and B.J.) is admiral, but it is at the same time wholly unrealistic.

Am I saying that you should stop trying to be like the greats? Of course not. We should always continue to chase perfection—and in truth, the elites are still on the same chase—but we should also be honest and realistic with ourselves. When my body began to break down and I had to work a fulltime job while also giving time to the love of my life, I realized that I could never be B.J. Penn, and that was a hard realization to accept.

Now, some three years later, that realization has actually increased my enjoyment of jiu-jitsu. I am no longer trying to be B.J. Penn or Marcelo Garcia. I am trying to be the best Marshal Carper possible. I still learn as much as I can from the elites, but I am not beating myself up over not winning Pan Ams or not earning my black belt in three years.

I can focus on making the most of the resources that I have, my time and my body, no matter how limited or flawed they might be. And it's more fun that way. My goal is not to be the best competitor in the world. My goals are to be as technical as I can and to be as good of an instructor as I can. And those goals suit me, because I have also set goals for my career and for my family that are just as important to me as my jiu-jitsu goals. There is nothing wrong with not being a world champion professional jiu-jiteiro. Have fun, and nurture the other parts of your life, especially your relationships.

2. Accept that Only You Think Jiu-Jitsu is the Most Amazing Thing Ever

I have noted a strange evolution, or rather devolution, in my own romantic relationship. After consulting with other committed jiu-jiteiros, I have confirmed that this trend is nearly universal and transcends jiu-jitsu.

Caris, my soon to be wife, began our relationship with an incredible admiration for my wit and intellect. When I spoke, she clung to every word and looked at me all starry-eyed and smitten. Everything I said was scripture, and Caris found it immensely interesting, whether we were talking about politics or jiu-jitsu. As time progressed, the awe faded, but her interest remained. Then she steadily began to challenge and question my statements until we reached the point where I was a little boy arguing with an adult about adult ideas, saying silly things and living in an imaginary world where my thoughts were substantial even with a Sippy cup in my hand.

For the most part, I had been unaware of this gradual shift in our relationship until one summer evening. I had been pondering a particular side control escape for some time, turning the position over in my head and working out hypothetical scenarios and leverage points. My fellow jiu-jiteiros are familiar with this process. We casually meditate on a position for days, the problem lingering in our brains. We analyze it during lunch and in the midst of meetings. It stays with us like some religious riddle, never quite leaving our thoughts.

And then we have an idea, a solution, and we do not want that eureka moment to fade back into the darkness of the jiu-jitsu unknown. We have to try our new technique, and we have to try it now.

So, on that summer night, I had a minor epiphany, and I needed a training partner. I triumphantly strolled into our bedroom, congratulating myself on my discovery. Caris sat on the bed, preparing to paint her nails.

"Can I borrow you for a second?"

"What for?" she answered, not looking up.

"I need to test out a technique."

Caris dug through her bottles of nail polish and selected a bottle. Mermaid Tears, a sort of turquoise. "Just go over there," she said. "I'll watch you."

Cue trombone zoom. Her words transported me back to 1991. I was four and standing in our backyard. Bowl cut. Those baggy multi-colored pants that looked like physical incarnations of *Saved by the Bell* title sequences. I held a glass of oddly colored chunky liquid.

After watching a marathon of Disney's *The Gummi Bears*, I was determined to replicate the recipe for their super bouncing potion Gummiberry Juice. I was certain that mixing wild blackberries with sugar, Sprite, Coca Cola, blue berries, and chocolate syrup would grant me the amazing Gummi Bear bouncing powers. This was the moment, the point where I would finally have a super ability.

If you were born in the 90s, and I am sure that some of my readers were, you may have missed the excellent cartoon that was Disney's *The Gummi Bears.* The premise: the Gummi Bears are in hiding after humans destroyed their civilization, desiring their magical abilities and technologies. Centuries later, the Gummi Bears are thought to be mere fairytale, but humans occasionally stumble upon Gummi-Glen, where the Gummi Bears live, and a group of ogres are hunting the Gummi Bears as well. The ogres want the Gummiberry Juice, which gives Gummi Bears magical bouncing abilities and gives ogres super strength.

Gummi Bears probably sounds like a pretty weird show, and it was. For a show founded in the 80s, though, Gummi Bears was relatively tame. The same decade produced *ThunderCats*, *Denver the Last Dinosaur*, *Care Bears*, and *Fragglerock*. The creative process that produced 80s cartoons is shrouded in mystery, but know that lead paint was not banned in the United States until 1978. The writers and artists behind 80s television grew up in houses rife with lead paint, which causes "delayed development" according to Wikipedia. Mix delayed development with any drug of choice, and it's no longer surprising when a television show is based entirely on anthropomorphic turtles learning ninjitsu from an anthropomorphic rat in between pizza runs in the sewers of New York.

The weirdness of my cartoon viewing had not yet occurred to me. At the time, I was much more interested in magic abilities. I yelled into the house through the open window to my dad, who had helped me gather ingredients and told me what berries not to eat.

"Dad! Dad! Come drink the Gummiberry Juice with me!"

He called back, "That's okay. I'll watch you from here."

He watched *Baywatch* instead, and the Gummiberry Juice failed. I didn't bounce. I puked.

With Caris, I had reached the final stage of devolution. I was a little boy again.

Jiu-jitsu is like Gummiberry Juice. You think it's amazing, and it makes you feel awesome, but not everyone in your life will have the same rabid passion for it as you do, especially when you have been telling them about it for years. Just because your significant other tires of hearing about jiu-jitsu does not mean that your relationship is in danger or that your love is weakening. He or she is probably just tired of hearing about your favorite hobby. Give your significant other a break, and talk about something else.

3. Take Time Off

Jiu-jitsu is a long term commitment, which is a lot to ask of yourself and the people that also want your time. We have already addressed the idea of contenting yourself with being the best you possible, rather than comparing yourself to the professional grapplers that can train all day every day. On that same note, taking a night or two off from training to stay in and watch four hours of *Game of Thrones* is okay. If you watch just one episode at a time, you lose the momentum of the intrigue and betrayal. And if you play the drinking game where you take a drink every time Joffrey is a douche, you will only get moderately buzzed if you stop at a single episode.

Now that we have Netflix, DVR, and box sets, we can watch television shows in nine hour eye-bleeding binge seasons. No commercials. No waiting a week between episodes or waiting six years for an all-day marathon on a television network that nobody watches. You can just keep hitting next over and over, losing yourself in whatever universe houses your show of choice. Ten episodes of *Scrubs* in one sitting? Sure. How about a three-day marathon of *Cheers*? Go for it. A start to finish endurance run of *the Sopranos*? Might be a bad idea. After three seasons of the Sopranos, you will refer to percentages as points and plot to establish your own shylock empire.

Time-off is important, both for your television viewing and for your relationship, and it is ultimately good for your jiu-jitsu as well. If you establish a routine of always training on certain nights, opting to spend time with your wife or husband instead of training demonstrates that you are in fact committed to them, and that you are happy to sacrifice for them. You're a true jiu-jiteiro, gladly choosing to not train is a big deal. Anyone that has spent enough time with you, like your significant other, will know and appreciate that fact.

By balancing your life and nurturing areas that are not jiu-jitsu related, the people in your life will be more supportive of your passion, making it easier to train consistently and for longer.

The Office Challenge Match

Spend enough time in the streets, and you will eventually find yourself interviewing for and landing a job. The streets are tough, and if you have any hope of surviving them you have to find a way to pay your jiu-jitsu tuition and buy a fancy limited edition gi that is produced in the same Pakistani factory that produces the more affordable gis, you will seek out a career or a profession of some sort. Fortunately, the streets lead to your job, and though a sliding glass door lies between you and the asphalt that you call home, every technique that you have learned for the street is just as practical in the office. Little do your coworkers know, a thick layer of concrete is hidden just beneath the industrial-grade carpet. Concrete is a close cousin to asphalt. Asphalt's dad is tar, and his bother—concrete's dad—is a lazy, good-for-nothing low-life that turns into a pothole after two weeks on the job.

While you are at work, you will encounter your own version of Trooper Scott or Office Aikido Guy. Doubters are nothing new to a jiu-jiteiro, and we already dedicated an entire chapter to troubleshooting the verbal attacks of naysayers. A challenge match, however, is a different beast entirely. A challenge match is not a casual insult directed toward jiu-jitsu that implies that you would lose in a fight. A challenge match is an explicit attack on you and your abilities that clearly states that a physical battle should occur between you and the issuer of the challenge.

Since dialect and accents vary from region to region, here are some examples of what a challenge match might sound like:

"I challenge you to a battle of fisticuffs to prove that your jiu-jitsu is inferior to my Receding Hairline Kung Fu."

"Fight me. You will lose."

"We should arrange a match to determine who the better fighter is."

"My penis is bigger than yours."

"Fuck you."

When it is clear that a challenge match has been issued, tradition says to schedule a time and a place for the event with but one exception. If a challenge match is ever issued on a beach in Brazil and one of you is wearing a speedo, the challenge must be resolved immediately. Honor whichever tradition is appropriate for the setting, which in this case, because you are in an office park, is to schedule the challenge match for a later date. Pick a time that is convenient for both you and your challenger, and choose a location that is somewhat private and not easily accessible to law enforcement.

Next, shake hands with your challenger because this is the last time that he will ever look you in the eye.

The most effective techniques for a challenge match may surprise you. A challenge match is about more than winning. A challenge match is about honor and about pride. You do not simply win. You must dominate your opponent. You must break his spirit and shatter his ego. When a challenge match ends, your opponent will know for the rest of his life that you are his superior. He will see your face in his dreams and in the shadows. He will never forget the biggest mistake of his life: challenging you.

You should not use your guard or look for armbars or triangle chokes. You should approach a challenge match like it is a fight to the death, an old timey colonial pistol duel. For example, consider America's seventh President, Andrew Jackson.

In a duel against a talented marksman named Charles Dickinson—the attorney, no relation to the writer or to Kermit the Frog—Jackson decided that he could not win by speed. His opponent was simply too good with a pistol. Instead, Jackson's plan was to allow Dickinson to shoot first, in part because he planned to play upon the phallic nature of his opponent's name by making a premature ejaculation joke at Dickinson's expense and because dueling etiquette forbade either party from moving until both had fired their guns. Jackson hoped that Dickinson would be so nervous that he would miss, giving Jackson plenty of time to take aim and win the duel.

Jackson was wrong. Dickinson shot him in the ribs. But Jackson was a tough bastard. He aimed carefully at the motionless Dickinson, ignoring the bullet in his chest, and killed him.

Do not shoot one of your coworkers. That's not the part of the story you should be paying attention to. Nor should you be focusing on the juvenile penis jokes. You should, however, learn from Jackson's cunning. After all, outsmarting your opponent is a big part of jiu-jitsu. Outwitting your opponent is the key to true victory in a challenge match.

At the time of your challenge match, schedule a same-day delivery of weightloss products, gym memberships, and plastic surgery brochures to arrive at your challenger's home. Address the delivery to his wife, and include a card that says, "These gifts will help us fix the problems in our relationship." Sign the card with your challengers name.

It is said that Masahiko Kimura had originally planned to use this move to win his challenge match against Helio Gracie but instead decided that it was too cruel. In Kimura's honor, use this technique with discretion.

The Americana vs. The Americano

To review:

Americano: *single or double shot of espresso combined with 16 oz. of water.*

Americana: *lateral keylock known in judo as ude-garami (arm entanglement) also known as a figure-four armlock.*

The difference between an Americano and an Americana may still be confusing, despite the above definitions, especially since they sometimes overlap in the wild. Take this scenario for example:

You are in Starbucks, or better yet you are supporting your locally owned artisanal (here at Artéchoke we love all things artisanal) coffee shop. The sun is starting to rise, and you are schlepping off to your craptastic job, jonesing hard for your caffeine fix. Brain foggy, eyes barely open, but the anticipation is building. Your mouth waters, your fingers tingle, and your heart palpitates. Your entire body longs for the java buzz. You are number five in line, then number four. . . three. . . two. . . Just one more to go and then… It happens. It's him. Again! This cannot be, not again, not today! You have reports to file, and you have already been late three times this month.

Damn! It's the Coffee Douche.

Barista: "Hi welcome to (insert name of overpriced coffee shop here). What can I get started for you?"

Douche: "Yeah, can you tell me what's in a coconut-carmel-mocha-latte?"

Barista: "Sure it's three shots of espresso, coconut, Fijian mocha extract, and angel tears."

Douche: "What can you tell me about where you source your milk? Is it from grass fed, hormone free, free-range cows? Are your coconuts from Thailand? Is it real or artificial? Are the angel tears organic?"

As the minutes of this exchange tick on, you find yourself and the others in line growing restless. Your anti-coffee-douche teammates murmur and gasp in frustration. You check your watch, and you see the point of no return approaching. With 15 minutes left in your commute and 5 minutes to park and 3 minutes to army crawl under your boss's window, you have only 4 minutes to get coffee. You wait. And you wait. You panic. You cannot afford to be late again. A junky twitch overtakes you, a nervous shaking coupled with uncontrollable blinking. "Damn it man! Make a decision already!"

If you are late, you must face another lecture on life priorities from your superiors and, worse yet, you will have to work late, which means missing the advanced gi class. No! Your heart races, terror and rage consume you, and the woman behind you pulls out her mobile and dials angrily. Chaos is imminent. You must act fast to save yourself and those around you. You have been training for a moment like this. A moment where you can stand up and right a wrong. Make a difference. Breakout from the "silent majority." Be a hero. But how?

What jiu-jitsu technique will protect the innocent and preserve the peace? A rear naked choke? A kneebar? A berimbolo? You decide to wait. Violence is not the answer here.

Then you hear it, it cuts through the palpable tension in the air like an arrow.

Douche: "As long as your coffee is fair-trade, shade-grown organic, I think I'll just have an Americano."

What? An Americano! It took him 5 minutes to order two shots of espresso cut with hot water! Seriously!?

You are pissed. The people in line with you are pissed.

Violence is definitely the answer. You look around and check the belts of everyone in the room. Yep, you outrank everyone here. It is up to you to put your training and skills to good use and right this injustice.

Americano. Americano. Americano. The word echoes in your mind as jiu-jitsu awakens your body, a rejuvenation greater than any caffeine rush. Americano... Why just last week we were reviewing the.... That's it! We were reviewing the Americana!

Prepare to get your Dockers™ dirty. It's time to serve this coffee shop villain a hot cup of retribution, compliments of the everyman, 40hr/week, working-stiff who just wants to order an overpriced cup of hot water and beans in a timely manner. You hand your cellphone to the woman behind you and tell her to start filming because what you are about to do is going into your tournament highlight reel. You crack your neck. You loosen your arms. You tighten your belt. And you bow.

At least that's what you imagined would happen. The more you train jiu-jitsu, the more likely you are to fall victim to these sorts of daydreams. You are not alone. The average jiu-jiteiro will experience multiple jiu-jitsu daydreams in a given day. In your mind, you will double leg waitresses, rear naked choke political analysts, and helicopter armbar annoying coworkers.

This is normal. Jiu-jitsu changes how you percieve the world around you, and it teaches you a new way of solving problems. However, these fantasies should never manifest as actual physical violence unless your safety is threatened. Instead, vent your frustrations to your jiu-jiteiro support group. They will understand, and they will help you maintain your sanity when you are away from the mat.

The Coffee Douche, with his trucker hat and vintage camera, insists on berating the barista with little concern for the quickly growing line behind him. Darryl sticks up for the everyman and politely asks the Coffee Douche to complete his order. When the Coffee Douche becomes unruly and aggressive, Darryl takes the fight to the ground and finishes the Coffee Douche with an Americana, an ironic end to an ironic man.

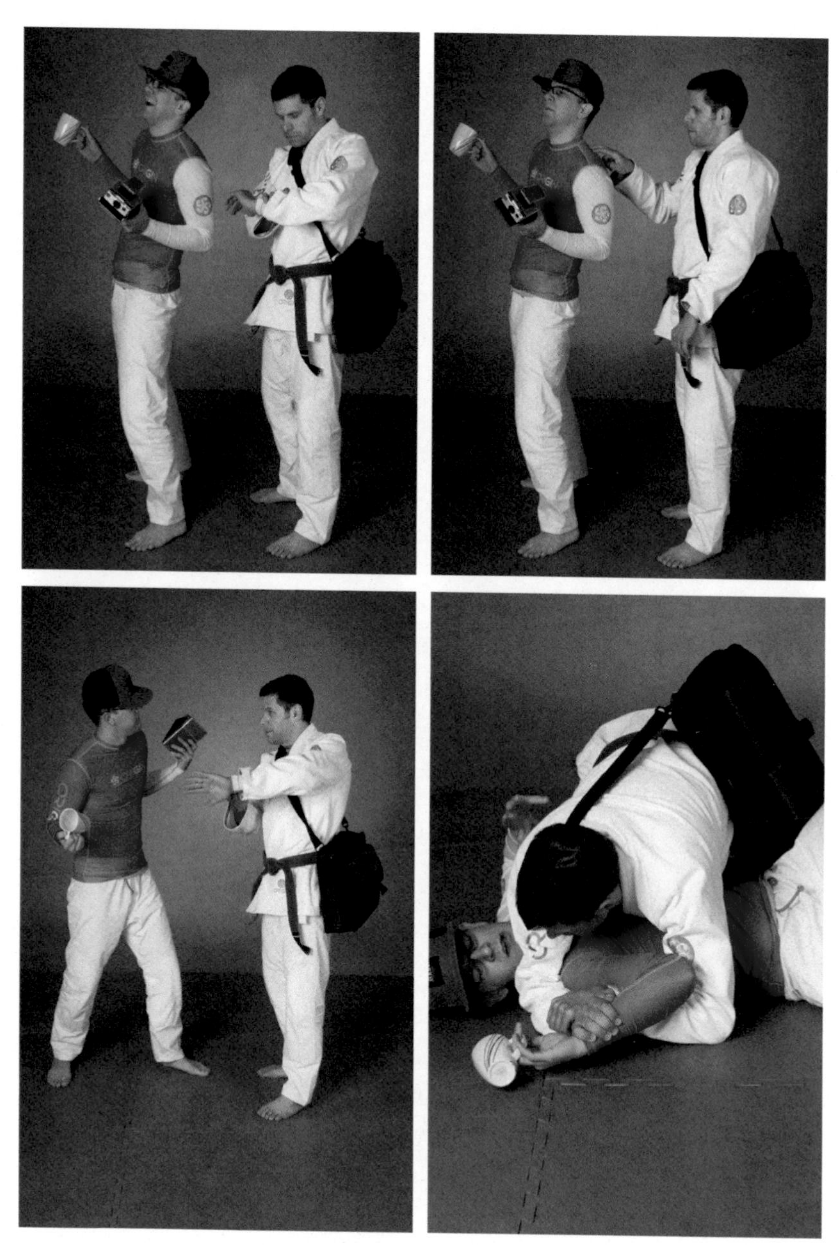

Good Posture on the Mat & In Your Life

Posture. From grade school on it seems we are always reminded of the importance of maintaining posture while sitting at our desks, standing in line, or swinging a bat. For many of us, however, posture is something that we take for granted. Unless we are having major back pain and are told by a healthcare professional to arrange our work-space for better ergonomics, most of us tend to let our posture slack while sitting at our desks or driving our cars (since Marshal and I are chained to our desks for 40 to 60 hours a week, we think about ergonomics as often as we think about jiu-jitsu). Most of us, though, don't bother to pay attention to our posture, ever. In general, we have become a culture of "slackers," and I'm not talking about the flannel wearing kind who were cool in the 90's.

I see a lot of people who let their shoulders slouch, their backs hunch, and their heads droop as if they're carrying the weight of the world. This Quasimodo phenomenon is as common as pimples at a Beiber concert.

With so many of us feeling overworked and overextended, scrambling to make ends meet, it's easy to understand why so many people present a "posture of defeat." We are too emotionally beaten to keep our backs straight and our heads high. Our attitudes are defeatist and negative and few of us are willing to look the world in the eye and face the day head-on.

Reasons for justifying pessism abound. It's easy to want to bury our heads, get lost in the shuffle, and keep looking down.

And this has everything to do with jiu-jitsu.

First, foremost, and most obvious is the need to maintain good posture while you roll: If you have ever rolled against a jiu-jiteiro with a tough closed guard, you know how hard it can be to avoid getting broken down and swept. Keeping your back straight, your weight distributed evenly, and your gaze looking up can mean the difference between getting submitted and making the pass.

As my close friend and jiu-jitsu instructor Jimmy Dent likes to remind me (and quite painfully so), the instant your opponent uses his guard to pull your head forward and bend your spine, you are in trouble. There are few things worse in jiu-jitsu then allowing your opponent to continually break your posture. Even if he is not setting up for a submission, he is forcing you to expend precious energy, and you are left to fight both your opponent and gravity to regain posture. When you're caught playing this game, it's only a matter of time before you find yourself losing position.

This same principal is true for standing guard passes or facing an opponent playing open guard. You must keep your back straight, your head up, and your hips forward.

Though we often talk about posture within an opponent's guard, posture is essential in all jiu-jitsu positions.

For example, many jiu-jiteiros like to play the seated guard or "butt-scoot" position. This is a favorite of both Marshal and myself because of the many effective sweeps and counters that can be achieved from this position. However, one aspect of this guard that's commonly overlooked by new jiu-jiteiros is the importance of butt-scoot posture. In order to be effective from this position, to not get pushed over onto your back, you have to keep your back straight, but that is trickier than it seems.

Your weight should always be centered, never leaning backward or sideways or forward. From the butt scoot, this means positioning your chest over your legs and scooting your butt out behind you. If your posture is weak, your opponent will simply push you over, but if your posture is correct, your center of gravity will be strong and his attempts to push you will be ineffective.

It should be clear to you now just how important good posture is when it comes to developing effective jiu-jistu technique, and I belabor the point of posture in the butt-scoot position to illustrate the importance of considering posture in all scenarios, even in places where you may not conventionally think of its importance.

It is just as important for this principal to carry over into your "off the mat" life. If you are reading this, chances are you are already practicing or maybe thinking about starting to practice Brazilian Jiu-Jitsu. This is something to be proud of and not something that everyone can do. For this reason alone, you should pull your shoulders back and lift your chin.

Most of us who practice jiu-jitsu have no delusions of becoming a world champion, nor will many of us enter the cage to become a mixed martial arts superstar. Most of us are just average, everyday, hardworking people looking for personal fulfillment.

If practiced in the right environment with the right people, jiu-jistiu can be immensely rewarding. It can provide us with an outlet for our frustrations, an active meditation where we can clear our minds from outside distractions and focus on the moment at hand. At it's best, jiu-jitsu can teach us that for every bad situation we find ourselves in, there is a counter and maybe even a re-counter, a seemingly endless variety of ways to improve or maintain our position both on and off the mat. And just as it's important for us to maintain our posture, whether we are passing a guard or presenting a radical idea in a corporate meeting.

I was in my mid-30s when I started training BJJ. I hit a point several years ago where life was beating me down personally and professionally. In the span of a few months, I was in bad car accident, my wife had a major, life-threatening health complication, and my business hit a rough patch. I felt as if life was spiraling out of control. I started to lose interest in favorite hobbies, like snowboarding and biking. I was tired. I felt defeated. My head hung and my back hunched.

During this time, I had a conversation with a good friend who happens to be a lifelong martial artist, and he encouraged me to start training

Karate again, something I had started when I was 16 and had done on and off throughout college. At the time, soon after I first started Karate, my dad passed away. At 16, I wasn't emotionally equipped to deal with losing a parent. It would have been easy for me to go off the rails and become a total fuckup. However, Karate played a big part in helping to keep me grounded by raising my self-esteem and providing a positive atmosphere to let out my frustrations. As a result of the positive outcome of my early experience in the martial arts, I felt that a return would give me the boost I needed to get through the shit that life was dumping on me.

When I first walked into a jiu-jitsu class, I wasn't sure what to expect, but it didn't take me long to realize that it was one of the best decisions I could have made. Beyond the physical and mental challenge, the fun, and the comradery, jiu-jitsu has taught me to face my fears, keep my head up, to maintain my posture, and to not let an opponent or life break me down.

The more time you spend on the mat, the more you begin to see the mat as a lens, a new way of looking at life, the universe, and everything. Just as you imagine hip-tossing random bodybuilders at Dairy Queen, you can't help but to begin thinking of life in jiu-jitsu terms. Jiu-jitsu, and Marshal and many other jiu-jiteiros would agree with me here, can help you to become a better person.

The lessons we learn on the mat can give us a new perspective and lease on life. On the mat, where problems tend to be much simpler than they are in life, you can break a problem into basic components. If you enter a match with a poor attitude, you are more likely to lose. If you do not dedicate yourself to your training, your progress will be slow. If you achieve a dominant position but do not make the effort to secure and hold your advantage, your opponent will exploit a weakness in your technique and undo all of your work.

You can see how these lessons can affect our views on real-life challenges, but in the moment, when life is whirlwind shit-storm, you can forget these simple lessons. Having the mat to remind you is a powerful thing, and it did wonders for me.

So the next time you're on the mat, at the bus stop, or in the board room, remember your posture, because you're a jiu-jiteiro, and jiu-jiteiro's relish a challenge.

Opposite Page

(flower sweep posture): As Darryl stands to break Marshal's guard, he steps and leans forward, comprising his posture and his base. Marshal quickly capitalizes on Darryl's mistake by hooking Darryl's leg and executing a flower sweep to secure the mount position.

(butt scoot to drag single): Stepping forward to pass Marshal's seated guard, Darryl leans forward. Marshal counters by dragging Darryl forward, transitioning into a back-take as Darryl falls face-first into the mat.

(proper butt scoot pass posture): In this photo, Darryl keeps his back straight, which centers his base over his feet, making it difficult for Marshal to yank or drag him.

(proper butt scoot posture): Marshal demonstrates posture in the seated guard. His feet are flared, the outer edges digging into the mat to allow for quick movements forward or backward. His elbows are inside of his knees, and his hands are over top of his feet and near his collar so that he can swiftly and easily counter grip attempts. His chest is forward, hovering over the space between his legs, to center his base, making it difficult for an opponent to tip him backward. And lastly, his head is up, strengthening the stability of his spine.

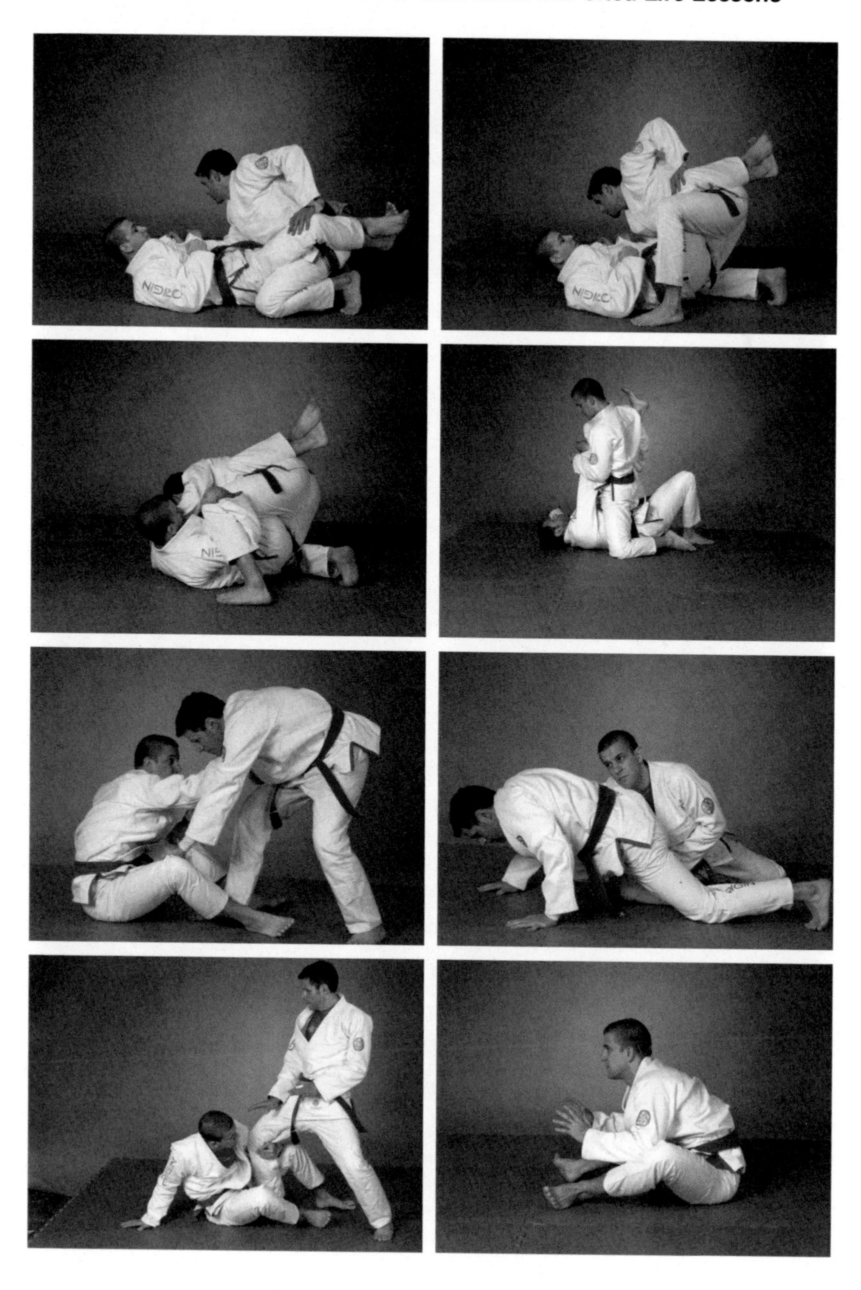

Two Secret BJJ Techniques that Your Instructor is Afraid to Show You

Brazilian Jiu-Jitsu is a complex art. Two bodies can become entangled in seemingly infinite combinations, and the presence of the gi makes the art even more intricate as possibilities continue to multiply. Even as jiu-jitsu engineers continue to perfect and invest in new mat technologies like the berimbolo and deep half, some techniques have been deemed too dangerous by the Jiu-Jitsu High Counsel and have been forever banned from use in competition, in the gym, or in the street. The Counsel feared that these techniques gave too much power to mere mortals, and that humanity simply could not be trusted to use these techniques exclusively for good, so they locked the techniques away, vowing to keep them a secret for all time.

Before the publication of this book, only a few jiu-jiteiro's knew of these techniques. Most of these individuals hold a seat on the Jiu-Jitsu High Counsel, and while their identities are a secret, our sources indicate that many of them share the same last name: Gracie. Outside of the Counsel, only two other individuals are confirmed to have learned the two lost jiu-jitsu techniques. You may know them as Barack Obama and Lady Gaga. The power of the lost techniques was too much for Lady Gaga to bear, and it quickly corrupted her spirit and filled her with peculiarity. Though she has used the power exclusively for financial gain, she continues to spiral into madness.

Obama, however, approached the two lost jiu-jitsu techniques with respect and wisdom. He read the sacred texts only once and then locked them away with national security secrets and nuclear weapons access codes. By foregoing the process of drilling and mastering these techniques, Obama was able to protect himself from their corrupting power while still giving himself a failsafe. By familiarizing himself with the techniques, he could identify when they were being used against him or his nation. Were that to happen, Obama would then risk his soul by learning the lost techniques so that he could use them against his attacker.

As I said, this was all before the publication of this book. I share these secret techniques with you now because they are no longer a secret. Wikileaks published them in one of their information dumps, and it is only a matter of time before a nefarious world power discovers the files and ascends to total domination. I beseech you, my fellow jiu-jiteiro, to cleanse your spirit and approach the following techniques with a pure heart. If you feel that you are not fit to carry this burden of knowledge, please pass over the next few pages lest ye be plunged into blackness. You have been warned.

The Belt Rank Soul Suck

Above: Marshal encounters an attacker on the street. Acting quickly, he unties his belt and strikes with a whip-cracking motion. Since Marshal outranks his attacker, his chi is able to overpower his attacker's soul, absorbing his life force and forever trapping it in Marshal's belt.

Lobstering

Marshal attempts to shrimp out of side control, but Darryl's pressure and control is too great. Marshal begins his transition to the legendary lobstering technique by reaching into his gi. Marshal removes a trained Brazilian attack-lobster and sicks it on Darryl. Darryl begs for a quick death as the lobster tears at his flesh.

The Definitive Guide to Pulling Guard in a Crowded Club

In this section, I'm going to reveal to you one of the greatest and most sought after secrets in all of Brazilian Jiu-Jitsu: How to pull guard in a crowded club. As jiu-jiteiros, we often hear about how if we used guard at the bar, our attacker's cronies would kick our head in with their stylish shoes, or we may end up landing in a puddle of Miller beer and bad decisions. These are legitimate concerns, but they are overblown.

The guard is a versatile position, and if you approaching pulling guard with the right mindset, you can escape all of these dangers.

The technique itself is quite simple, but for many it's initially very difficult to grasp. However, if you can get your head around just three guiding principles, or "rules," you will have this mastered this much-debated technique.

Are you ready?

You might want to sit down. This experience will rival the feeling of seeing Royce Gracie land a submission for the first time in the Ultimate Fighting Championship.

The first rule of pulling guard in a crowded club is...

DO NOT PULL GUARD IN A CROWDED CLUB.

The second rule of pulling guard in a crowded club is...

DO NOT PULL GUARD IN A CROWDED CLUB.

The third rule of pulling guard in a crowded club is...

SEE RULES ONE AND TWO.

Now, let's break that down one more time from a different angle:

If you find yourself in an altercation while in a crowded club, a dive bar, a locker room, a shady street corner, or if you're being attacked my an axe-wielding madman…

DO NOT PULL GUARD.

Further more:

Do not butt scoot and start playing seated guard. Do not attempt spider guard, or butterfly guard, x-guard, rubber guard, high guard, or the "Daedric Guard of Invincibility" (unless you're a level 75 battlemage). Under no circumstances should you intentionally attempt to "play" any type of guard in a self-defense scenario.

Use your guard when necessary. Otherwise, make like a selfish lover and stay on top for as long as you can.

No one ever told you to pull guard on the street. No one. There is no legitimate BJJ instructor in the world who teaches his students to attack from guard as the first reaction to a self-defense situation. "Guard" as the name implies is a defensive position. It is a valuable and indispensible tool to any jiu-jitsu practitioner, but it's intended to provide the means to improve position in a bad situation.

Only one man has ever made pulling guard in a street fight perfectly viable. His legendary abilities are partly to blame for the lingering misconception that jiu-jiteiros want to use their guard in a street fight. This man was so successful at it that others tried to copy his techniques. When they failed—dropping to the seated guard to set up an arm drag only to be blinded by a war pig upskirt—the reputation of jiu-jiteiros wanting to play guard began to grow.

His name was O Scootarachi. His story: infamous.

"A Lenda do Scootarachi"

Some claim he descended from a tribe of butt-scooting warriors who lived deep within the Amazon rainforest. Others say that he was the result of a clandestine Cold War era initiative between the C.I.A. and the Gracie family, an attempt to sweep the scourge of Communism from South America. Then there are those who maintain that he was a simple açaí farmer, so heartbroken for his beloved who died at the hands of an Argentinian drug lord that he sought only vengeance. They claim that his rage burned so deeply, that he traveled into the jungle and spent years honing his guard like the edge of a machete against a whetstone.

While no one can be certain of his origins (or the origins of his oddly Spanish sounding name[1]), what is known is that from Leblon to Ipanema to Barra to Rio, everyone knew to both fear and respect this master of the seated guard, this jiu-jiteiro excelente, this lobo solitário.

It is said that "O," as he became known to the people, was so proficient in his guard play that he could clear out an entire bar from seated guard using only his hooks, all the while never spilling a drop of his caipirinha.

Tale after tale tells of how the mighty Scootarachi vanquished foes by setting a single hook. One account claims "O" used what can be described as an early prototype of the berimbolo to defeat a much larger champion sumo wrestler who had travelled to Brazil to challenge him. Another story tells of a fateful night in Copacabana when Scootarachi used de la Riva hooks to disarm a diamond-wearing gunman while defending the honor of a local showgirl. To this day, however, historians debate who swept who.

Bar after bar, club after club, favela after favela, O Scootarachi scooted, swept and arm-dragged his way to become the stuff of legend.

---

1 Gringo, they speak Portuguese in Brazil.

A true hero of the people, a veritable "Robin Hood of the Inside Hooks," O Scootrachi achieved an admiration from the people of Brazil rivaled only by their admiration of Pele, Formula One drivers, and Santos Dumont[2] .

Children of all ages sang songs, told stories, and dreamt of perhaps one day meeting "O Mestre do Scoot" in person. All Brazilians of a certain age have fond childhood memories of playing "Scootarachi e Gringos," which is similar to the American game of "Cops and Robbers".

Rumor has it that none other than Bruce Lee himself was so taken by tales of Scootarachi that he set out to make a movie based on them. It is said that the original working title of "Enter the Dragon" was actually "Enter the Scoot," but movie executives feared audiences were not ready for such an exotic hero.

An attempt would once again be made in 1982 by Hanna Barbera to bring the legend of "O" to North America with the production of an Americanized version of the tale in the form of a Saturday morning cartoon series "The Ultra Amazing Adventures of Scootarachi & Friends." It was cancelled after just three episodes. Not even the "gringo" twist of introducing a kid-friendly canine companion, "Cão do Scoot," was enough to make "O Scootarachi" palatable to an American audience that was still unfamiliar with the "Arte Suave".

In his controversial 1992 best seller "Scootarachi, mito ou verdade? (Scootarachi, Myth or Truth?)," renowned cryptozoologist Hans Klaab claimed to have uncovered ongoing attempts made by the U.S. government to locate and recruit O Scootarachi into service as part of a top secret "black ops" super-solider program.

---

2 Gringo, if you don't know who Santos Dumont was just ask any Brazilian "Who was the first man in flight?"

Klaab claimed that none of the U.S. agents who were sent to Brazil were ever heard from again.

Among Klaab's more controversial assertions was the claim that in 1980 a U.S. official travelled to Rio prepared to offer "O" a large sum of money if he would agree to help the government end the "Iran Hostage Crisis." That official returned to Washington with a broken arm and nice sun tan.

Perhaps Klaab's most controversial claim, one reviled by American conservatives, was that it was "O" and not Ronald Reagan who was responsible for bringing down the Berlin Wall. Klaab said that he had photographic evidence taken on November 9, 1989 that showed a shadowy figure butt scooting along the top of the wall. He claimed that this same shadowy figure was later seen "seated" at the base of the physical and political divide, digging his feet into its foundation.

As Brazilian Jiu-Jitsu's popularity spread throughout the world, so too did "A Lenda do Scootarachi". With more and more "gringos" flocking to jiu-jitsu gyms, more people were becoming enchanted with the intricacies of the guard, often to their own detriment. The admiration for "O Scoot," often on a subconscious level, has clouded the judgement of many jiu-jiteiros, causing them to overlook some of the more practical applications of jiu-jitsu.

Perhaps if O Scootarachi hadn't overshadowd his lesser known and not nearly as beloved contemporary, Topo Jogo Gustavo[3] , more jiu-jitsu players would be enamored with the top game.

Alas, this is not the case, and therefore all jiu-jiteiros must develop "situational awareness" so that they understand when and when not to utilize their guard. For unless you are "O Scootarachi," the guard is not always your friend.

---

3 This my friends is a story for another time.

It is said to this day that if you're sitting quietly on a beach in Brazil and you listen closely you can hear the song of the Scootarachi on the wind, whishpering "The Legend of O Scootarachi." The man. The myth. Mestre do Scoot.

The next time you and you're training partners are hanging out in a bar or "crowded club," order a round of cachaça, and drink a toast to honor the legend. And if the meathead at the end of the bar wearing the tattoo shirt on top of his tattoos challenges you, do not pull guard.

On The Mat Wisdom

M

The walls of a jiu-jitsu gym are like a marble from Men in Black, it's a whole different universe in there, and it's very different from the universe you are used to. In jiu-jitsu gyms, the usual definitions of social rank and superiority are irrelevant. Looks, money, fame, and even biceps size are no longer indicators of status, which is great news for guys like me that have never had any of those things. On the mat, the most dedicated and the most skilled—which sometimes excludes the most talented—are the leaders. Jiu-jitsu becomes an equalizer. Can someone with more money afford to train more often with more people? Theoretically, yes, but we have seen enough rags to riches stories in jiu-jitsu to know that buying your way to excellence is not as easy one might think. To reach the top of the jiu-jitsu food chain, you have to be smart and committed, and it is on these two factors that you are primarily judged. I take comfort in this.

Not everyone, however, will find solace in this social reset. You get to start from scratch, yes, but you also have to learn a new set of social norms and develop a way to compartmentalize those norms so that you use them in the gym and not at In-N-Out Burger.

For example, bowing when you enter the gym is a common show of respect, but if you bow when you enter a fast food restaurant, you may be run over by the McFrequent-Flyer riding a Hover Round as she shrieks her excitement for a triple stacked burger in a language known only to the oldest, most ancient evils of Mordor. For reference, here are some other jiu-jiteiro specific practices that are only acceptable within the walls of a jiu-jitsu gym:

- Continuing your physically strenuous activity when your belt has fallen to the floor and the top half of your clothing is flowing in the wind like Fabio on a rollercoaster.

- Realizing that someone is bleeding on your clothes and shrugging it off.

- Twisting someone's arm behind their head like they just jumped out of an episode of *Cops* only to have them laugh and compliment you on how well you twisted his arm the wrong way.

- Game-planning ways to be more systemic and effective at intentionally and efficiently dismantling the human body.

Because jiu-jitsu is an usual sport—if you disagree, you are not being honest with yourself or your pajama-wearing friends—it attracts unusual people. Most of these people are perfectly harmless. They may be socially awkward, but they tend to be good people. In my training, I have witnessed the following strange behaviors:

- Smelling shoes before putting them on.
- Wearing a grass stained gi to training after a morning of practicing rolls in the backyard.
- The never-nude that refuses to change in the locker room.
- The exhibitionist that insists on changing just inside the front door.
- The guy that takes jumping jacks really seriously.
- The proud owner of an excessively large cup.

None of these behaviors particularly bother me. They just make me raise an eyebrow, and for the most part, that's how most jiu-jiteiros would react. There are, however, very specific behaviors that will earn you the ire of your clan or derail your progress. As a white belt, guessing at what to do or how to act can be an embarrassing process of trial-and-error—and I'm sure a few readers were like me and guessed at how to tie their belt and emerged from the locker room to be greeted by a sea of puzzled faces. Save yourself the heartache, and study the lessons from this chapter.

Top Then Ways to Be "That Guy"

Anyone who has spent more than a few classes on the mat knows what I mean by "that guy." That guy is the person that you avoid at all costs. Chances are most of the people that you train with feel the same way. In a strange way, some mat rats take pride in being that guy. They like the attention. They like the infamy. Jiu-jitsu has yet to determine why some jiu-jiteiros are drawn to being that guy, but studies have shown that every gym has at least one. If you desire to rise to the status of that guy, here are ten tried-and-true steps for securing your position at the bottom of the barrel.

10. Use the Internet.

Go to internet forums, and tell the other users how tough you are. Insult as many strangers as possible, and under no circumstances should you contribute to discussions in a constructive, meaningful way. Just mash your keyboard and mix in some obscenities. It's like ground-and-pound, except it's on the internet instead of beneath the leaky roof of a fairground pavilion.

9. Frown.

Do not bother shaking hands or saying hello when you enter the gym. Sit in the corner by yourself, scowling and wallowing in your greatness. Being a part of the community and helping to generate a positive learning environment is for people like Teila Tuli. Some Dutch guy kicked his teeth out. You don't want your teeth kicked out, do you? Yeah, I didn't think so.

8. Lie.

If you have never fought, competed, or trained, tell everyone that you have. If you are a real tough guy, you will order your belt online, leave the gym for a month, promote yourself, return, and tell your training partners that you were traveling and some guy with a Brazilian-sounding accent promoted you.

The only person you cannot lie to is your mom, unless she asks about the magazines under your bed. Lie about those.

7. Critique technique.

Even though you have only been to two jiu-jitsu classes, your UFC Fight Night collection makes you an expert. Do your classmates a favor and constantly evaluate and critique their every move, even if they have been training since before you knew that Royce Gracie was pronounced with an 'H' instead of an 'R.'

6. Bleed.

Leaving your wounds uncovered is not a danger to yourself or others. If you are going to put a band-aid over the cut on your foot, it might as well have unicorns and rainbows on it. Leave the wound to leak and spill. Your training partners will be honored to have been blessed by your plasma.

5. Skip the warm-ups.

If you come to class on time, not only will you fail to make a dramatic entrance, but you will be forced to take part in the warm-ups. Your natural athleticism cannot be improved by exercises and stretches, so come into class just as the warm-up ends. The alternative to this advice is to ignore the class warm-up and to instead do your own in a corner by yourself. If you choose the alternative warm-up, maintain eye contact with the instructor throughout.

4. Let your finger and toe nails run wild.

If you want to be an animal, you have to have claws. Trimming your nails is on par with shaving your legs. So what if the green rhinoceros horn growing from your big toe skewers your training partners? When they complain about the goring, they are really just saying that they wish that they could be as cool as you.

3. Treat every match like a death match.

If your partner asks you to go easy, maybe 60 percent, do his wussy-self a favor and give it everything you got. If you lose, you are less of a person, and everyone at the gym will whisper behind your back about how you had to tap. You do not want that. If Helio Gracie had big biceps, he would have used them. So grab that headlock and squeeze, squeeze, squeeze!

2. Hold submissions extra long.

If your partner taps, do not let go right away. Just as you wait through the one and two-minute teasers to get to your two-hour flick filled with action, guns, and nudity, so should you wait out the soft taps to get to the hard panicked taps often accompanied by yelling and cursing. Tough guys wait for the hard taps. Be a tough guy.

1. Never clean your gi.

When your noxious aura enters the room long before you do, you will know that you have officially become that guy. With your gear saturated with the sweat and grime from a month's worth of training, your training partners will be unable to push you out of their heads. Your musk will enter their hearts and minds by crashing through their noses like the stench of a bloated roadkill deer.

Bonus. Creep on your female training partners.

This last step is incredibly advanced, and it's not for everyone. If you want to make the jump from black belt to red belt, you need a technique that will trounce every other "that guy" move known to the first world. When a female comes to your gym to train, make her as uncomfortable as possible. Ask to work from her guard and from north-south. Sit awkwardly close to her on the mat. Invite her out for drinks after.

If all goes well, your behavior should turn her off to jiu-jitsu forever, and that's when you will know that your technique was effective.

A Step by Step Guide to Mat Hygiene

Because I have seen many man-gorillas take up Brazilian Jiu-Jitsu, I feel it necessary to review one of the core principles of modern civilization:

hygiene. Since the invention of germ theory, which ultimately originated around 36 BC but was not validated and established until the 1800s, humankind has known that germs exist and that they are agents of great evil. Fortunately, in most cases, germs are easily defeated with basic cleanliness. Cholera or the Bubonic Plague may not be a concern at your gym, but ringworm, staph, and other communicable diseases like the flu and the cold should be. Jiu-jitsu involves a great deal of contact in a warm, humid environment. With 30 people on the mat in any given class, and all of those people trading partners and sharing the same mat and locker room space, a jiu-jitsu gym is a germ's dream.

In fact, scientists have observed germs hitchhiking their way onto the mat. When a germ realizes that it has entered a jiu-jitsu gym, it gets a boner.

Mat hygiene demands a higher level of care than general day-to-day hygiene because of what is at stake. Ignoring your hygiene responsibilities puts your health at risk, the health of your training partners at risk, the health of their families at risk, and the health of the business as a whole at risk. Though they are somewhat rare, a staph outbreak can quickly spread outside of the gym, and many of your training partners are likely to have young children that they play with and hold. Your carelessness could harm more people than you realize, so take your hygiene seriously. Hold yourself and your training partners to a high standard. It's best for everyone.

If you happen to be one of the man-gorillas, whom I referred to earlier, that has no idea how to use soap or a washing machine, I have prepared an easy to follow step-by-step guide for jiu-jitsu hygiene.

1. Shower before and after a training session.

You should enter a training session clean and fresh, and when a training session is over, you should shower again as soon as possible. Do not wallow in your own filth. In the event that your job requires a fair amount of physical activity and involves dirt and sweat and perhaps other particulate matter, showering before a training session is recommended, both for health reasons and for the sake of your partner's nostrils. Spending an entire class drilling with someone that reeks of fermented perspiration is not enjoyable.

2. Brush your teeth.

Gingivitis may not be on the level of staph, and if you are concerned about catching someone else's gingivitis while training you are probably training at the wrong kind of jiu-jitsu gym, but bad breath is a serious problem. It paralyzes your training partners. It induces dry heaves. And the foul odor shrivels any hope of enjoying jiu-jitsu the way that a cloud of mustard gas sucks the life out of helpless sunflowers. By the time you are old enough to sign a waiver, you should know whether or not you are prone to bad breath. In the event that you do suffer from a case of mild or extreme halitosis, no one will hold it against you as long as you make an effort to manage it. Brush your teeth before training, use breath mints—anything you can do to keep your breath minty-fresh will help.

3. Wash your gi.

You should never wear your gi more than once without washing it. There are no exceptions for this rule. None. Absolutely not. Line-drying your gi after training does not count as washing. Leaving your gi in your trunk for three days does not count as washing. Spraying your gi with Febreeze, Lysol, or Axe Body Spray does not count as washing. To wash your gi, you must insert it into a washing machine. Add the recommended amount of detergent, your favorite fabric softener (lavender), and perhaps some borax or Oxyclean to fight odor and dinginess. Your gi must then go through a full wash cycle. Whether or not you choose to air-dry or machine-dry your gi after a wash cycle is up to you. However, your gi should be completely dry before you hit the mat.

4. Trim your finger and toenails.

Fingernails and toenails can be hangouts for germs and fungus, and the longer they are, the more likely they are to cut training partners and spread disease. Trimming your nails should be a usual part of your hygiene routine. Keep them short, and keep them dull. If you are a forgetful person, put an extra pair of nail clippers in your bag. That way, if you happen to notice your talons while you are changing into your gi, you can hop into the restroom for a minute to remedy the problem.

5. Wash your hands.

You may be okay with fondling your junk and making a sandwich with no steps in between, but your training partners are not. Wash your hands when you come into the gym. Wash your hands when you use the restroom. Wash your hands when you handle anything that might be susceptible to disease, like a bloody tissue used to clean up a nose bleed. Simple cleanliness will do a lot to maintain the overall health of your team.

6. Heal.

If you have a cut or scrape that cannot be managed with tape and bandages, take a week or two off and let the wound heal. Open wounds are susceptible to infection, and glossing the mats with your fluids is not sanitary either. If the bandage will not stay on, sit out, for your sake and for everyone else's. In the event that you have a cold or the flu or ringworm, stay home. Do not assume that you are not contagious because it has been a few days since you started your antibiotics, and do not assume that because you rubbed some antifungal cream on it that your training partners are safe. Wait until you are fully recovered to train.

Alligator Wrestling is Good for Your BJJ

Alligator wrestling is a form of exercise that until now has been the best kept secret of the south. Wrangling an alligator activates every muscle group and develops your core. The unpredictable nature of the alligator's natural defense instincts will improve your base and strengthen your stabilizer muscles. The movements in alligator wrestling mimic jiu-jitsu movements: you squeeze with your entire body, and hip movement is essential. After six weeks of alligator wrestling, you will feel the difference on the mat. You will be stronger, faster, and more confident in your balance.

For the low low price of $499.00, you can have the three DVD set, a pair of alligator wrestling shorts complete with confederate flag embroidery, and three adult alligators of varying weights, so whether or not you are a beginner or a veteran, you can start alligator wrestling today (alligator care equipment not included).

Sound familiar?

Replace alligators with kettle bells, balance balls, yoga, P90x, Pilates, CrossFit, Ginastica Natural, barefoot running, powerlifting, swimming, altitude training, or gymnastics, and you have a much more familiar sounding claim: train this thing to be better at jiu-jitsu. Every year, a new super routine rises to popularity, and less-experienced jiu-jiteiro's rush out to buy DVDs and equipment. When Andre Galvao published a book full of drills and released a few YouTube videos of him performing some impressively acrobatic balance ball exercises, balance balls rolled into gyms everywhere. As much as we may not want to admit it, we all gave it a try, and most of us fell flat on our faces. It was hard not to try, though. Galvao is such a good grappler, and every jiu-jiteiro longs to be on that level. If a balance ball helped to get him there, then sign me up.

And that's how it starts. Those of us that get swept away by training fads have our hearts in the right place. Our passion for the sport, though it keeps us dedicated and motivated, ends up working against us when it comes to the latest and greatest in mat science.

Lifting weights or running barefoot or wrestling alligators will not make you better at jiu-jitsu. Doing jiu-jitsu will make you better at jiu-jitsu. There is no way around it. No short cuts. No warp whistles.

Does that mean that you should give up on your CrossFit training or your yoga? Not at all, but be realistic about the benefits and about how you balance your training. Strength, agility, flexibility, and speed are valuable attributes on the mat. Exercise is always good, and improving your health overall can have a positive impact on your training. And if you enjoy it, all the better, but do not expect miracle improvements in your grappling ability. Having a bigger paintbrush does not make you a better painter.

If your training time is limited and you want to supplement mat time with gym time, do it. If you enjoy running just as much as you enjoy jiu-jitsu, then divide your free time between the two as you see fit. Your free time is yours to do with as you like, so do whatever makes you happiest. If jiu-jitsu is your only passion, and for many people this will not be the case, any activity that cuts into your mat time will slow your progress. If you have to give up a training session to make it to Pilates, you are hurting your jiu-jitsu more than you are helping it.

Never Tap Again... 7 Secrets to winning the Ego Game

When you play the Game of Egos. You win or you die... well. . . you win or you tap. You might die if he doesn't let go, or if that weird heart condition that runs in our family (the one usually activated by llamas) strikes from the shadows in the midst of a clock choke. But anyway.

His belt, you want it so bad you can taste it. Your shoulder may be hurting, but fuck that noise! Your instructor is watching, and if he sees you hold out against this "advanced" guy's submission "attempt" he'll obviously promote you, probably at the end of this class.

Now your shoulder is feeling like something's about to tear. Block out the discomfort and that strange crackling and popping as well, and remember, pain is what jiu-jitsu is all about. You're a modern day gladiator, and this gym is your ludus. There is no practice. Every training session is your Mundial. Some of these pussies around the gym talk about taking it easy and going 80 or sometimes even 70 percent, and we can pause to chuckle at that. Did you have a good chuckle? A nice hearty belly laugh? Good. Moving on: you, don't go easy! It's 125 percent or bust.You will hold out no matter how many submissions he attempts.

But wait. That triangle just got a bit tighter. Don't worry about it. The worst that will happen is that you go to sleep. Update: he is combining his triangle choke with an armbar. It kind of hurts. Scratch that, your arm is about to break, and everything is going dark. . .

Tap tap tap.

Your manhood is shriveling, and your girlfriend is leaving you. Your family will shun you.

It's time to reset. No worries, you got this bro-heim. You need a strategy.

What will it be? The quick hand-shake to arm drag? The "I'll act like I'm going to take-it-easy then once he goes to guard unload at 155 percent to yet again contradict the meaning of 100%?" Or the "slap hands and jump on his head?" Yes, that's it slap hands and-well damn. Swept again.

Now what? This cat may move like a 9-limbed orangutan on the ground, but those 6 months you spent training Tae-Krav-Do-Ryu-Kido made you a stand-up powerhouse. If only you could stand him up...But you can't and you seem to be stuck.

And he's on your arm again.

Fuck it! You don't need to use that arm anyway. You can still do curls with the other one. Plus, chicks will dig seeing your arm in a sling when you're out at the clubs. Give yourself a pat on the back bromo-sapien; you could've tapped, reset, went another round, maybe asked your opponent for some pointers, learned a thing or two, but really in the end what's that get you?

Look at you now sitting atop the Ego Game. Everyone is sure to respect you now. You may miss the next 4-6 months of training, but that's nothing compared to knowing that like so many brave warriors before you, you refused to tap! You are tough. Like really, really tough, 'cause like you know, you didn't tap. Chicks will love hearing that.

Do you want to be this tough? Below are 7 Secrets to Winning the Ego Game:

1. Intensity, Intensity, Intensity.

Gentle art. Ha! You want to win - be aggressive. Come out hard and finish panting and wheezing every time.

2. Gut it out.

Caught in a choke? Starting to gurgle? Hold on. Blacking out isn't so bad. There's no risk of serious brain damage if you come around within

30 seconds.

3. "Master is Tricksey."

That little gray dude knew what he was talking about. Tap hands and jump on a bitch's head. Tell them "I'm a little tired so I'm just gonna go light." Then unleash a 6-pack of awesome on them. Tell them that you have an injury and ask them to be careful about taking your back. If they sweep you and are about to mount, feign an injury.

4. Game Face.

Seriously, what's up with all this friendly shit? Intimidate. Scowl. Eye of the tiger baby. These are not your friends. This is combat. Look tough, never smile. Ever.

5. Lift: A lot!

Preferably before class. If your pecs are massive they'll never be able to pry your arms loose for an arm bar.

6. Master the Internet.

The more videos you watch online the more techniques you'll have to trick (see secret #3) your enemy combatants. You all learn the same moves at your school or gym, what's up with that? Who needs instructors when there's a whole Internet full of techniques that are probably better?

7. Let them have it.

If you're caught, or rather if that brown or purple belt sort of has the submission, sometimes it's cool to give a quick tap and tell them that you "let them have it." You know, just so you don't totally destroy their self-esteem. If you're the same rank or they're just some blue belt, you can always tell them it was a stalemate and you tapped because you needed to get a drink.

Above: Master is very"Tricksey" indeed.

So there you have it bro-dacious…7 tips to becoming a true playa`.

Author's note: All of these tips are derived from research and interviews, not from personal experience. We had to hire a team of wildlife experts and animal psychics to conduct these interviews with a stable full of mat animals. We can't tell you what gym our sample is from, but we'll give you a hint: their fighters always promise,"I don't see this going out of the first round" in pre-fight interviews.

D

A Good Start, In Life and On the Mat

It's 6:30am when the alarm on your smartphone blasts you awake to the timeless melody of Wu Tang's "Protect ya Neck." Groggy, your eyes mere slits as your hand fumbles around your nightstand, groping for the phone, you manage just enough finger dexterity to hit snooze. Ah, sweet relief as you put off the inevitable for another 10 minutes.

40 minutes later, after repeating this cycle four times, the Gza's voice somehow sounding more angry as if he knows you're procrastinating, panic sets in as you realize your margin for error to get to work is now razor thin. You put one foot on the floor, stepping on your dog's tail while the other foot catches in the sheet. You fall out of bed like a drunk off of a bar stool. Your significant other, who has the luxury of being able to sleep in until 8:00am, gives you an annoyed look as he or she rolls back over for more sleep.

Tired, sore, and aching for caffeine, you start your day feeling like you've been on the receiving end of an American Top Team knee-on-belly seminar. After sitting in traffic, you arrive at your desk 30 minutes late, with all the enthusiasm of a bus full of hippies at a Slayer concert. The tone for your day has been set, and it's not a good one. You're behind, and you're going to spend the rest of your day catching-up. If you're good, or lucky, you may end up on top, but most likely you're going to end the day exhausted and unproductive.

Contrast this with how Marshal starts his day. He's stirred awake by the soothing island rhythms of Dennis Brown. Calm and relaxed, he efficiently rolls over his arm, practicing an imaginary side control escape. Caris, his fiancee, immediately makes an attempt to sweep him before he's able to get out of bed (Marshal has Caris act as Cato to his Pink Panther, helping to keep him ever vigilant in his quest for jiu-jitsu excellence). Undaunted, he thwarts her attempt and makes a smooth, effortless transition from bed to solid ground.

Alert, focused, and ready to take on the world, Marshal has a cup of coffee, sits at his computer, and begins another day of writing and jiu-jitsu awesomeness. Marshal brings this same starting-panache to the mat. He begins every roll like Kasparov on Ritalin... with laser focus and a sound strategy. Always proactive, he immediately gets to work, setting the stage to control his opponent and take the match where he wants it to go.

For most white belts and a lot of blue belts, a solid starting strategy is something that's either overlooked or incredibly frustrating. Many of us fall into the bad habit of allowing our opponent to dictate the pace of the match by being reactive instead of proactive. This is bad, man. While you may get away with taking a reactive approach against a less-skilled opponent, a veteran jiu-jiterio will exploit your hesitation. Once a skilled fighter has you in a weaker position, the odds of them making a mistake or leaving you an opening to escape are slim. It's like giving an Olympic sprinter a 3 second head start; you're going to get burnt like cheap toast.

The following are examples of some the most common mistakes novice jiu-jiterios make when starting a roll:

Deep Collar Grips

Whether you're starting on your knees, standing up, or in guard, as soon as your opponent gets a deep grip on your collar, you're in danger. A deep collar grip will allow your opponent to control your posture. If your opponent possess a "kung-fu" grip, you will look and feel like a child trying desperately to break free of his kid-leash. Instead, never let your opponent clip the leash in the first place.

Jimmy Dent, our fabled jiu-jitsu mentor that used to host a podcast called *the Lockflow Show*, often told me stories of his time training in the remote jungles of Brazil and of how most of the high-level jiu-jitieros started every roll by immediately reaching for a deep collar grip, attempting cross chokes with one foot still on the starting line. "Protect ya' Neck Grasshopper" was his oft repeated mantra to me when we trained, especially as he wrapped my lapels around my windwipe like the rope of a tetherball.

Foot on the Hip

If you're a jiu-jiterio who allows their opponent to place on his hip when attempting to pass open guard, stop this immediately. A foot on the hip is like a cross collar grip on your pelvis. It kills your posture and stfiles your movement. Once you allow your opponent to establish solid contact with your hip, he can have a leg-up (literally and figuratively) for the rest of the match.

Hooks

Like the above scenario with the foot on the hip, allowing your opponent to establish a butterfly hook is dangerous. Butterfly hooks, despite their whimsical name, are hard to shake. Someone who is good with the butterfly guard will off-balance you, leaving you susceptible to sweeps.

Assertiveness

Calm assertiveness is just as effective on the mat as it is on dogs. If you go at your opponent with a weak, half-hearted attack, it's going to fail, and when it fails, it will probably be epic. Jiu-jitsu is not a slot machine. You can't just throw techniques like you're slinging a one-arm bandit, hoping for a jackpot. Throwing out a technique without conviction sets you up for a loss.

Approach your opponent with a plan, and put solid effort into making that plan work. Set the tone for the roll by committing. Impose your will. Do not count on your opponent to make a mistake; set him up to make a mistake.

At the start of a match, unsure of how to proceed, Darryl pauses to Google a solution. Darryl should have had a plan, like fighting for a particular takedown or initiating a guard pull, as Marshal demonstrates.

M

The Legend of the DVD-Only Masters

A few years ago, I arranged for Matt Kirtley, an Eduardo De Lima black belt out of Clearwater, Florida, to give a seminar for a university martial arts club in the Pittsburgh area. Before the seminar, over a plate of sushi rolls, we discussed jiu-jitsu, because that's what jiu-jiteiros talk about. For this reason, you should be very careful about inviting too many jiu-jiteiros to a party. Before you know it, half of your party is discussing the latest Mendes brothers DVD set and the other half of the party is trying to hang themselves with party streamers but the cheap cray paper just keeps ripping every time they try to make a knot.

Matt and I weren't at a party. The only person that we were alienating was my fiancee, and she's used to it, so the jiu-jitsu talk continued.

As expected, we started talking about the new Mendes brothers DVD set. Matt and I are both information junkies, and Matt has made a name for himself doing technique research for his blog Aesopian.com, comparing the approach of one jiu-jiteiro to another, scouring the web and the dusty corners of Budo Videos for footage.

"Some people really take the instructional thing to the extreme though," Matt said.

I raised an eyebrow. I was a video junky for years. Had I gone overboard?

"I never told you about the guy's at Leo's?" he asked.

Matt proceeded to tell me the Legend of the DVD-Only Masters, a tale that had been told to him by Leo Kirby. To ensure the accuracy of the story, I went to the source and asked Leo if I could share this cautionary anecdote with the world, or the five people that accidently bought this book because of Amazon's one-click ordering.

Leo, like most of the jiu-jitsu world, learned of Marcelo Garcia after his performance in the 2003 ADCC, the tournament where Marcelo put Shaolin to sleep. Leo bought the ADCC DVDs and, with his friend John, studied Marcelo's game. He was a purple belt at the time. Two years later, Marcelo taught a private seminar in Miami and Leo scored a slot. After the seminar, Leo made it his mission to bring Marcelo to South Florida. The word Leo used was "conspired," which is Leo's way of saying that he became a genuinely good friend of Marcelo's. It worked out.

"When Marcelo finally moved, he didn't have a gym yet, so he invited me and John to train with him in his garage," Leo said. "We did that for 3 months, bringing my son and sometimes inviting another person. It was an incredible experience to be training with him in that small group at his home. He ran those classes just as seriously as he does his own gym."

When the real gym opened three months later, Marcelo didn't scale back the intensity.

"I guess it would be like having Tiger Woods to play golf with every week if you are a golfer. It was great. The intensity of the classes was unimaginable," Leo said. "He rolled every night with as many people as possible. One of the things I learned from him is how important it is to roll, a lot. I know there is always a debate between rolling and drilling, and we did both, but I think rolling is always the most important thing to Marcelo. There would be a couple of nights that we skipped the technique section and drilling, but we never skipped rolling. We always rolled."

Marcelo eventually moved back to New York, which left a void at Leo's gym.

"During the two years that he was in South Florida, as you might imagine, we attracted a lot of very competitive students," Leo said. "They trained hard and they trained often, and they wanted to compete at the highest levels. Many of them left when Marcelo did, and I don't blame them."

Some of the students that stayed wanted classes to be run the way that Marcelo ran them, but the Marcelo class style appealed primarily to the intense competitors. With the intense competitors gone, the gym needed to pull from a more casual demographic to keep the business alive.

Leo kept the situation in perspective, saying, "Jiu-jitsu, in the end, is an individual endeavor, and you need to train the way you want to train, but there were issues when a couple of guys wanted the class to be run one way, and John and I, as the instructors, were going to run it our way. From Marcelo's point of view, he always said that we were the instructors and that we should do what we thought was best."

The compromise that Leo, John, and these students reached was this: after the regular class, they could run a class their own way. They brought a laptop, a television, and a subscription to MGInAction.com. They ran a Marcelo-style warm-up, cozied-up to the screen to watch a technique, and then drilled it. The entire class ran that way.

"I think that's fine for a couple of guys training, but to run a class like that just makes no sense to me. And incidentally, it didn't make sense to Marcelo either," Leo said.

The Legend of the DVD-Only Masters spread around Florida, earning Leo some unwanted attention. As word spread, the gym continued to divide, reaching the point where there were two factions under one roof: the students that trained with Leo and John, and the students that trained with Marcelo in spirit via MGInAction.com.

What Leo experienced was an extreme case of instructional infection. Nearly every jiu-jiteiro catches a minor case of it at some point in their career, typically at white belt when their immune system is weak. The common cold equivalent of instructional infection manifests as late nights of watching YouTube videos and just a little too much Crack Head Control for a no-stripe white belt.

"The real issue in my mind," Leo began, "was that, if we were a Marcelo

Affiliate, we wanted to teach Marcelo's game, but that meant his entire game. John and I were the only ones there who had trained with Marcelo even before he came to the United States. Anyone who knows Marcelo knows that he constantly changes his game, but I think he builds his game on things he can already do, and I have always thought it was important to understand his entire game, not just the things he was doing since he came to Florida.

"Here is an example: All of his students who have trained with him in the last 3 or 4 years are great at the one-legged X-guard. But many of the guys I have trained with are not that good at the regular X-guard. Knowing the evolution from the regular X-guard to the one-legged X-guard helps you with both games. Marcelo started using the one-legged X-guard because opponents began trying to keep him from getting an underhook on their leg to set-up the regular X-guard. But he could do the one-legged X-guard with an overhook on the leg. So now he could get the sweep. Being able to go from one-legged X-guard to X-guard and back is important I think."

The moral of the story is that instructionals are powerful training supplements, but they can't connect all of the dots for you. Your instructor provides a powerful perspective that cannot be replicated with any book, DVD, or service. Again, instructionals are amazing, and at Artechoke Media we are big fans of their ability to share information with jiu-jiteiros around the world, but the human element is the core of jiu-jitsu. Treasure it.

In Leo's case, the culture at of his gym has since shifted dramatically, and the DVD-Only Masters have moved on or seen the light that is jiu-jitsu fundamentals, taking classes from Leo and John. And the culture has evolved to cater to tough competitors, casual new students, and the older guys that are passionate but want to train at their own pace.

Now that you have heard the Legend of the DVD Only Masters, it is your duty to pass it on to the next generation so that the story—and its moral—never dies.

Rubber Guard and Deep Half Guard Tips for White Belts

Jimmy Dent, one of my instructors and good friends, a brown belt at the time but likely a black belt by the time you discover this book in the 25 cent section at the adult bookstore yard sale (with the pages stuck together for some unknown reason), used to hold question/answer classes. Instead of picking a topic and teaching three or four techniques, he took questions from the class. His reasoning was that it was nearly impossible for him to guess what positions his students needed to learn most, so asking them directly would accelerate their learning and boost their ability. Or so he theorized.

I, however, had never actually seen him teach a class like this. It sounded like a group private lesson and a great chance to solve my current jiu-jiteiro problems. I asked him when he planned to run another class like the one he had just described.

"Never," he said.

"Why not?"

"The last time I tried it, someone asked for options from crackhead control. So I broke down the position and demonstrated some attacks and transitions that you could use from there. When I walked around to see if everyone understood, I saw the same student that made the request sucking ass setting up rubber guard. I told him to think of crackhead control as another form of high guard, and he looked at me and said, 'What's high guard?'"

Jiu-jitsu is an exciting sport. The possibilities of positions and attacks seem endless, and you customize your style to fit your body and your preferences. As a white belt, entering that new world is overwhelming. It's exhilarating. And it's empowering. You want to learn everything. Now.

And, naturally, the latest jiu-jitsu technology is the most attractive. Rubber guard. Deep half. Fifty-fifty guard. The berimbolo. World champions are raving about these positions online, and they are using them to win the biggest tournaments in the world. In a comparison of coolness, the berimbolo will always trounce the scissor sweep. The scissor sweep is your 1995 Ford Escort. Yeah, it starts, and it's mostly reliable. It will get you from point A to point B and back again. But the radio only picks up AM stations. The windows are manual. And you are pretty sure your back seat doubles as a stray cat brothel when the sun goes down.

The berimbolo is the Fisker Karma. Haven't heard of it? That's the same way most jiu-jiteiros reacted when the word "berimbolo" started floating around jiu-jitsu forums, and no one could decide how to pronounce it. The Fisker Karma earned *Esquire Magazine*'s award for 2012 Most Gorgeous Debut Car of the Year. Henrik Fisker is a former Aston Martin designer who launched his own car design firm in America. The Fisker Karma is his baby, and *Esquire* described it as "polarizing, gutsy, and a little unbelievable." It is the sexiest hybrid in the world. Sleek. Shapely. The body seems to ripple like the muscles of a wild animal and the curves beckon like a siren.

Ask someone to choose between a Ford Escort and the Fisker Karma, and he will choose the Fisker Karma every time. Except that a Fisker Karma is not a car for new drivers. You would not toss the keys to your pimply good-for-nothing 16 year old and watch him as he backs out of the driveway and tears off to court Poison Ivy at Comic-Con. Not in a Fisker Karma. No. Even if he is a good kid, you give him a beat-up Ford Escort because he has a lot of lessons to learn and mistakes to make before he drives quite possibly the most beautiful car ever built. In an Escort, you can focus on getting there. Stakes are not terribly high. You can make a mistake or two parallel parking and get back to figuring out how to park, not figuring out how to find a repair shop that can service your gorgeously ridiculous vehicle.

At the white belt level, you should be focusing on the basics, the fundamentals of how and why jiu-jitsu works. Feel free to goof off from time to time and experiment with the newest grappling inventions, but do not lose sight of the importance of basic jiu-jitsu. Even Eddie Bravo, who catches a lot of flak for the complexity of rubber guard, openly states in *Mastering the Rubber Guard* that students should master the rest of closed and open guard before they learn rubber guard. The new stuff is built on the backs of the old stuff. Without the old, the new will not work. Bravo spent years training basic jiu-jitsu with Jean Jacques Machado. Yes, Bravo experimented with new positions and attacks in that time, but his foundation was tried-and-true Brazilian Jiu-Jitsu techniques.

The same can be said for Caio Terra, the Mendes brothers, and Jeff Glover. These grapplers have contributed a great deal to the evolution of jiu-jitsu, but they too started as white belts, and they too started by learning basic jiu-jitsu.

Injuries Ain't No Big Thing

As safe as jiu-jitsu can be, injuries are a normal part of training, as they are with any high contact sport. As Tyler Durden suggests, on a long enough timeline, every jiu-jiteiro will experience an injury. You may experience a minor injury, a major injury, or plurals of the two. Injuries can come early or late in your career, in the gym or in competition. You will get injured, but a talented jiu-jiteiro will handle the setback with grace. For an example of how not to handle an injury, see this anecdote from my life:

I tore my meniscus in three places and needed the end of my femur reshaped.

Did I get caught in a heel hook? No.

Did I catch my foot in the mat defending a takedown? No.

Did I sacrifice my joint to reach a new personal best at the squat rack? No.

I was in graduate school. I came back to my graduate assistant position after class, stomping the snow off of my pumas, ready to dig into some mindless database entry. My boss at the time played a major role in recruitment and often met with parents and families in his office. At the time of my arrival, a mother, a father, and their son sat at the table that doubled as my desk, talking to my boss about campus life and financial aid. He had set my laptop on the floor to make room for brochures and folders and handouts. As quietly as possible, I walked to the corner and crouched down to pick up my laptop.

As I dropped my butt to the floor, I felt the stability of my right knee shift, like my knee cap had slipped off track and jammed out of place. I kicked my leg straight, trying to pop it back in, but the knee remained locked at a right angle. I tried not to panic. I was on the floor, in my boss's office, and he was in the middle of an important recruitment opportunity. Yelling out in pain or asking for help would be awkward for all and leave a weird impression of the university for the potential freshman. I clawed my way to my feet, grabbing at chairs and desks and shelves, cripple-hopping to the closest office chair.

I tested the knee. It wouldn't straighten. It wouldn't bear weight. And it hurt the way the third *X-Men* movie hurt.

While the idea of another knee surgery and an indefinite layoff from training worried me, a more pressing concern worried me more. My car was in short-term parking, and my commute was an hour. I had to get my car home, and then I had to get to the hospital. The solution was obvious, and my coworkers took action as soon as the family left.

They wheeled me to my car in an office chair, past a crowd of undergraduates, down a long hall of classrooms with large glass windows, through the staff and faculty parking lot, through the paid parking lot, and to my car parked along the far tree line, the only free parking on campus. I did another cripple-hop out of the office chair and into the driver's seat. I fake laughed through the awkward stares, like I had just won an embarrassing bet, and I waived whenever someone pointed.

For the ride to the emergency room, I braked and accelerated through the pain and pounded the cruise control bottoms like I was setting the high score on *Street Fighter*. An hour later, I sat in my car in the hospital parking lot and phoned the front desk.

"Thank you for calling. This is Mindy. How can I help you?"

"This is going to sound strange, but could you send someone out to the parking lot with a set of crutches or a wheel chair? I need to go to the emergency room, and I can't get out of my car."

"Why can't you get out of your car?"

"I think I dislocated my right knee or tore something important. I'm not really sure, but I can't walk."

"And you are in your car by yourself?"

"Yes."

Mindy thought for a second.

"Are you there?"I asked.

"Yes," she said. "But if you can't walk, how did you drive here?"

"I'm in a lot of pain and could really use some help."

An orderly brought me a wheel chair and rolled me into the emergency room.

My orthopedic surgeon later told me that the tears in my meniscus had likely occurred some time ago but the angle of my squat just happened to be perfect enough to fold the cartilage over itself while the joint was bent, locking my knee at a ninety degree angle.

If I was manly and tough, my big injury would have occurred in the cage, at the hands of some bitter family rival. He would have latched on to my leg, and I would have looked directly into his eyes as he tore my joint to pieces, accepting my punishment for having made a silly mistake. Or, at the very least, my injury would have occurred in the gym during a tough drill. But not me. A laptop put me out of commission for eight months.

In the unfortunate event that you are injured in training or in competition, be thankful that your injury did not occur at the office in front of the resident Aikido expert. Visit your doctor, do what he says, and return to training when you are healed. No other course of action will protect your image. This advice applies to the full scope of injuries: broken finger, torn labrum, strained pelvic muscle, concussion, or ringworm. Follow your doctor's orders.

Seriously, do what the doctor says. Stop posting vague descriptions of your injuries on Internet message boards and asking for diagnoses and treatment options. If your doctor needs a magnetic resonance imaging machine to make an informed decision about your health, what makes you think that K3yboardSamurai69 will be able to tell you what's wrong after one poorly punctuated paragraph that says little more than "it's swollen and it hurts?" From now on, if someone on your favorite message board asks for medical advice, respond with one word and one word only. Cancer. It's definitely cancer.

And for the sake of jiu-jitsu, rest. Let the injury heal.

Here are some pictures that my doctor took during the surgery:

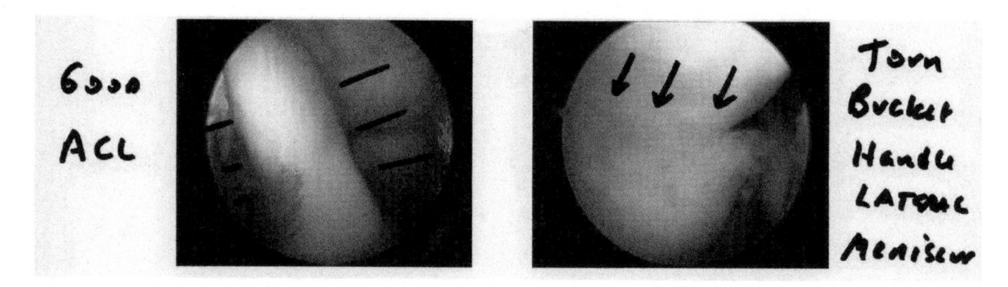

That sushi looking mass on the left is my ACL, and it's going strong. On the right, well, there's the problem. The cartilage is torn and folded over itself.

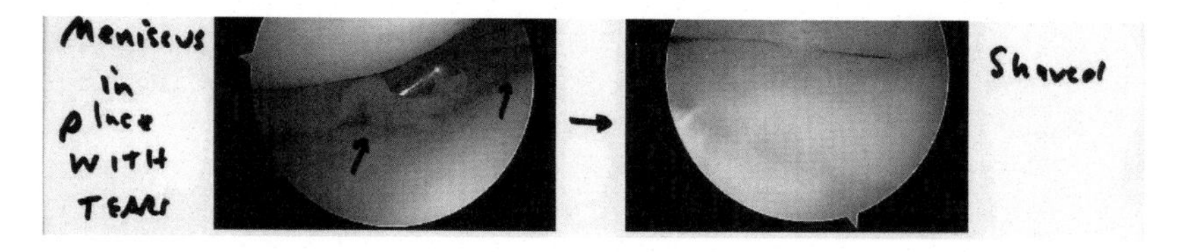

In this set of my photos, the surgeon has unfolded my meniscus and properly positioned the meniscus. As you can in the photo on the left, the edge of the cartilage is frayed. The photo on the right shows the cartilage after it has been shaved.

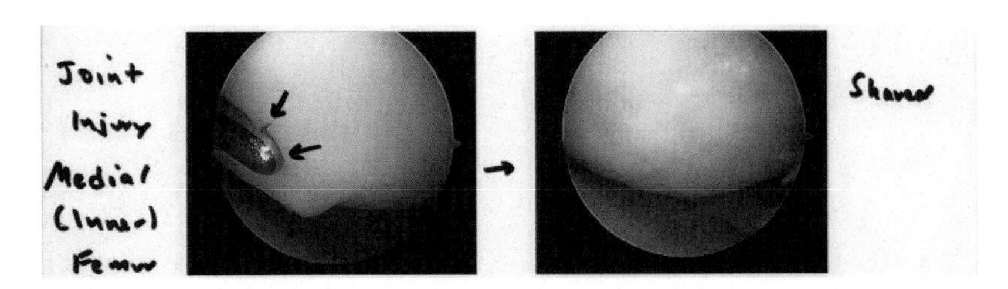

Pictured above is a bonus injury that no one expected. This is the tip of my femur, and the photo on the left shows that it's been chipped or damaged in someway. I blame Sit and Be Fit on PBS. Pictured on the right is my femur post-makeover.

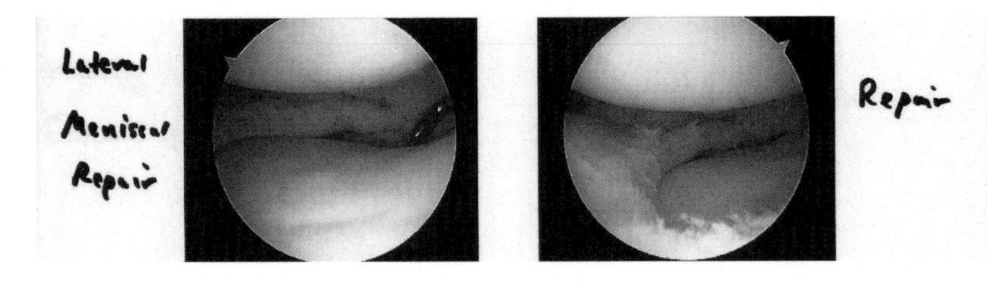

And this last set of photos depicts yet another meniscus repair. I hope that everyone enjoyed this journey inside of my body (thank you for the very fast Facebook responses). Does this mean I should bring a camera when I make that special visit to the doctor when I turn 40?

Paleo Jiu-Jitsu: A Caveman's Guide to the Arté Suave

While paleontologist's opinions vary, most accept that some time during the late Paleolithic era a split occurred with the evolution of jiu-jiterious and other early grappling hominids. There is no consensus on why or where the split occurred, all that is left are the fossil records and surviving grappling lineages on which to base this hypothesis. What we do know is that this split has left us with three distinct styles of jiu-jitsu: Brazilian or Gracie, Lucha Libre, and Caveman.

You made the switch to the Paleo Diet, and you traded in your Nike Air Maxes for a pair of Vibram Fives. You ditched your modern ways and went completely (and I mean compeltely) old-school. Overall, you have never felt better. Your Crossfit performance is up, and you are totally ripped with unbelievable stamina. Dragging rocks, throwing hammers, and flipping tractor tires have not only made you strong, but have also provided you with the skills necessary to rescue Uncle Rhabdo should he and his internal organs have another life threating encounter with farm machinery. As an added bonus, the money you save by not buying deodorant allows you to buy plenty of pasture-raised, free-range meat. Living like a caveman kicks ass!

If you could only start applying your prehistoric pimpness to other aspects of your life, like say for instance your jiu-jitsu game, your transformation would be complete. Is it possible? Can you go totally prehistoric on the mat and win? Well Ogg, break out some hormone-free, grass-fed jerky, throw Bronty a bone, add some wood to your cave fire, and master these seven techniques that will take you from Barney Rubble to "Mightor" faster than you can invent the wheel.

Lesson 1: The Guard

Cavemen hate playing guard, and they hate trying to pass guard even more. When it comes to the guard game, cavement don't fuck around. When passing, they like to keep it simple. If they have a club[1], they try smashing their opponent in the face. If a club is not available, they cross-face. If the club, the cross-face, and the heel hook fail, the resourceful cave-bro will go for the "pick-up and slam," grunting loudly (not to be confused with a kyai), lifting his opponent like a deer carcass and slamming him to the ground like he is proudly presenting his kill to a potential cave-girl mate.

A true caveman will avoid fighting from his back at all costs, but sometimes it is unavoidable. In such cases, a caveman will rely on a closed guard, a very tightly closed guard. We're talking as tight as humanly possible, tighter than a sabre-tooth's bite (which is way and I mean like way tighter than anything to come out of Brazil, accept for maybe the butts on those Zumba girls), with no pretense of moving to an open guard. Squeezing with all their might, a finesse-inspired cave-bro might attempt a cross-choke, but a beefcake cave-bro, the truest of all cave-bros, will just go for an ultra-gnarly neck crank, reaching up, grabbing their opponent by the ears and twisting like they're pulling the skin off a freshly killed hare (cave bros don't waste time on rabbits).

Lesson 2: Standup

When standing, a caveman attacks quickly and aggressively. The particular genus of the given cave-bro typically dictates what happens next. If you are a cave-bro, you should refer to your personal genus to determine the best course of action. If you are training to fight a cave-bro, you should research their origin to better understand their instinctual combat inclinations. The genus 'Homo Wrestlarus Brutum' will usually

1 Some schools frown on this and don't allow clubs on the mat. Always check with your head instructor before wielding a club.

take a shot, aiming for a hard and fast single leg. 'Homo Judo Playerus Maxis' will gird their loins, summon all their strength, and attempt a throw. While the genus 'Formerarus Footballus Lettermanus' will usually go for a spear or improperly executed double leg[2]. 'Neocrossus Fitorum' will typically attempt an Olympic lift, usually the snatch, but some slower members on the genus can only pull off the clean-and-jerk, hoisting their opponent into the air to slam them.

Lesson 3: Side Control

Cavemen love having the stronger position, even during practice with their fellow teammates. Cavemen especially enjoy side control. When cavemen have side control, they smash. Not pressure. Smash. Cavemen do not care if they leave space for their opponent to retain guard or to turtle. They only care about the smash. Occasionally, a more skillful cave-bro will move from side control to north-south where they can chisel away at their opponent's ribs like a recently felled zebra.

Escaping side control for the true cave-bro is a no-brainer. Bench press. They let their prehistoric instincts kick-in (like when a tree falls on you while hunting and gathering). They flex. They groan. And hair sprouts on their chest as they press their opponent into the air.

Oh, and remember: only sissies worry about getting caught in armbars. Cavemen smash their way out of those too.

Lesson 3a: Tips for perfecting the bench press:

1) Do not train legs.

2) Always throw the bar when re-racking it.

3) It doesn't matter if you touch the bar to your chest. Half benches with more weight look way more impressive to

---

2 The above is not aimed at the truly talented former athletes, wrestlers, judoka who apply genuine skill and crossover techniques to the standup game.

Darryl, frustrated by Marshal's closed guard, draws his caveman club and prepares to strike.

impressionable junior high students.

4) Leer at the ass of the hot babe on the treadmill between sets. This will increase testosterone production.

5) Chalk up before every set. Lots and lots of chalk.

6) Never go light. Never. Not ever. Light is what you drink when you're hanging with your cave clan and trying to cut carbs for the upcoming beach season.

7) Grunt and scream while blowing out that last, ultra heavy, back arching set.

Lesson 4: Taking the Back

Cave-bros love to take the back, but they are also impatient and uninterested in the whole "technique game." A true prehistoric pillar of brodacious awesomeness will jump on or over their opponent's head immediately after shaking hands. In the wild, this technique is used to

Caveman Darryl ponders whether to slam Marshal or to drag Marshal back to his cave and share the kill with his tribe.

outsmart wild boars, stone age pythons, and war pigs. It is an incredibly effective technique on the mat and in the street. If successful in taking the back, a cave-bro will usually cross his feet and squeeze as hard as possible.

Lesson 5: Mount

Cave-bros love all top positions, mount included. When cave-bros have mount, they, you guessed it, smash. As stated earlier, patience is not a defining characteristic of the true cave-bro, so establishing a technical base and methodically working toward a submission is not part of the prehistoric gameplan. Instead, a caveman who is truly stoked to have obtained the superior position will sit on their opponent's chest, exhaling the putrid scent of that morning's kill directly into their opponent's mouth. From there, some cave-bros like to go for the cross-face, while others prefer to suffocate their opponent with their huge rippling pectorals. Some fancy cavemen will on occasion look for a choke, but these cavemen are often shunned by the core of the clan. Since cave-bros typically obtain mount against smaller, weaker, less skilled opponents, this approach to mount is immensely successful.

Cavemen hate to get mounted because they cannot tolerate feeling inferior or weaker than any living creature. When cavemen are mounted, they revert back to the tried and true technique from Lesson 3 and rage through a bench press.

Lesson 6: Open Guard, Seated Guard, X-Guard, Spider Guard

If you thought for even a moment that a caveman would use a position like spider guard, you are not fit to join the clan. Obviously, you're some kind of metro-sexual that grooms and does yoga instead of not-shaving and dragging rocks.

Lesson 7: Submissions

Ogg see arm. Ogg attempt to crank on arm. Ogg see neck. Ogg attempt to crank on neck. Ogg have club, Ogg smash. Ogg on top, Ogg smash!

Ogg no tap. Ogg no recognize when other man tap. Tap weak.

Darryl, instead of shrimping or achieving posture, unleashes a guttural grunt and uses all of his might to bench press Marshal away.

Ogg strong. All submit to Ogg!

If you've read this chapter and you're thinking to yourself "This Caveman style sounds like just the thing for me..." do us all a favor: put down and the book and quit reading.

For the rest of you, if you've been training for any length of time, chances are you've encountered a full on cave-bro out on the mat. You know, "that guy." Despite ongoing evolutionary efforts on the part of the human race, the cave-bro is not going away. Jiu-jitsu can civilize many of them, so there is hope, but remember to protect yourself when you roll. You never know if a new student is a cave-bro or if on your training partners is a closet cave-bro.

Darryl, after clubbing Marshal to near-unconsciousness, grabs Marshal's wind-pipe with both hands.

Darryl, realizing that he is much stronger than Marshal, opts to abandon pursuit of position and technique, choosing instead to yank Marshal's arm out of its socket as though he were ripping a sapling from the earth.

The Shake Hands Arm Drag and the Partner Bow Back Take

Have gi, will travel.

It's true. With the ever-growing popularity of choking friends and strangers in a waiver-proofed environment, a jiu-jitsu gym is never far away, especially in major cities. If a legitimate instructor cannot be found, you can drop into the closest YouTube certified dojo and wreck the natives to boost your self-esteem. In either case, training is almost always an option. If you are going to be out of town on business or on vacation, pack your gi just in case. You may want to decompress after an all-day conference, or you may want to escape the mother in-law that invited herself on your family vacation. Never go anywhere without your gi. Ever. You never can tell when a jiu-jitsu session will break out, and you do not want to be stuck doing no-gi in your Abercrombie & Fitch jeans.

Be warned: not every gym will be as welcoming and as friendly as your own, even within your own organization. After years of traveling, neither Darryl nor myself nor anyone that we have talked to can identify any consistent pattern or warning signs that can be used to identify an unwelcoming jiu-jitsu gym. Beyond avoiding gyms that focus on mixed martial arts—which are magnets for the kind of meatheads that stole your pogs and slammers when you were young—the best you can do is to call and email instructors beforehand, extrapolating the tone of the gym from his or her demeanor. Even then, every gym has "that guy," and chances are that you will end up as his training partner the one time that you stop by to train. The rest of the gym might be a jiu-jitsu oasis, but you will never know because you and Ogg have to spend the next hour drilling together.

It happens to everyone. Make a mental note of the experience, and try another gym the next time you come back to town.

At the same time, do not confuse competitiveness with douche-baggery.

If your belt is anything but white, assume that you are a yardstick. Everyone will want to test their skills against yours to see how their rank and experience stacks up against an outsider's rank and experience. Even the nicest grapplers have a hard time resisting this self-test. You have probably been guilty of it on occasion too. We all are.

Characteristics of a competitive roll: fast, aggressive, and intense.

Characteristics of a douche roll: unnecessarily rough, lack of regard for safety, dirty.

I am proud to say that I have had my ass kicked in competitive rolls across the United States. I have no problem losing to talented grapplers, regardless of their rank or affiliation. I do have a problem with poor sports, and my worst jiu-jitsu travel experience occurred shortly after I earned my blue belt. I was visiting a friend, an avid jiu-jiteiro, in a state that I will not name. Naturally, we set aside time from drinking and gallivanting to train. At the time, we were attending separate colleges, and he had not been to his home gym for over a year because he was away year round. He was unaware that the culture at the gym had shifted in his absence.

We dropped in for a class. Class went well, and free roll began. A four stripe blue belt with a mohawk grabbed me immediately and asked me to roll. We touched hands, and he launched himself at me like a flying squirrel in heat. An elbow connected with my eye, and a foot tagged my groin. He quickly outmaneuvered me and set a choke. I tapped.

I sat up and reached to touch his hand again to reset the roll. He shook my hand but did not release. He transitioned seamlessly from the handshake into an arm drag with the finesse of someone who had used that technique many times before. He again set a choke, and I tapped.

On the way from the gym to the beer distributor, I told my friend about what happened. He erupted in laughter.

"That guy was a dick," he said. "I bowed to him to start a roll, and he smashed my face into the mat so that he could take my back. If he tries that shit in Brazil, he'll get stabbed."

Neither of us has gone back since.

When someone visits your gym to train, behave like an upstanding jiu-jiteiro. It's best for you, your gym, and for the sport to make this the norm. In the event that you encounter a douche-iteiro, smile politely, thank them for their roll, and never bother with them again.

When Marshal and Darryl shake hands to show respect, Darryl cunningly crosses his fingers. As Marshal bows, to again show respect, Darryl smashes his face into the mat and spins to take the back.

Conclusion

We hope that you enjoyed this romp through the lighthearted side of the jiu-jitsu lifestyle. The topics changed quickly, like a night of rolling with the clock set to six-minute intervals, forcing you to jump from problem to problem in rapid-succession. And that's part of what we love about jiu-jitsu. We love the variety, the ever-evolving challenge of learning and applying technique against training partners of different strengths and styles. You win some, you lose some, and through it all you learn a bit more about your art and about yourself.

This book, like a roll at open mat, was partially experimental. We are testing content and presentation to find new ways to share jiu-jitsu with the world, to see what resonates and inspires. Artéchoke Media aspires to usher in a new era of jiu-jitsu publishing. The book you now read is the first of many projects that we have planned.

In the near future, we will release a free instructional that demonstrates the Artéchoke approach to packaging and sharing jiu-jitsu technique. We are excited to take this new instructional model, and we are even more excited to announce our first Artéchoke faculty member and his first book. In time.

Until then, thank you for picking up a copy of the first Artéchoke effort. Thank you for sharing it with your friends and training partners. And thank you for being an avid supporter of jiu-jitsu.

Acknowledgements:

Marshal and Darryl would like to thank Sonny Achille of Steel City Martial Arts for his support and for his instruction, and Chad Djubek of Primal Photographic for lending his time and expertise to this project. A special thanks to Hunter, Kelly, and Nora for reading early versions of this unusual manuscript. And, of course, thank you to jiu-jiteiros everywhere for making the jiu-jitsu community what it is today.

Marshal would like to thank his wife Caris for her love and his mentor Alan for his guidance and friendship.

Darryl would like to thank Melissa for standing by him all these years.